I0381549

SHHHHHHHHH

SMUT-MAKER

Mike Corrao ©2020

Designed by John Trefry
for **Inside the Castle**.
Text is set in Clarendon, a 19th century slab serif typeface used on the *Wheel of Fortune* wheel. Titles are set in Albertus, found on the title card of Stuart Gordon's 1995 *Castle Freak*.

ISBN 9781732797178

SMUT-MAKER is the 23rd book from **Inside the Castle** and is a text in the expanded field of literature.

MAKER

INSTRUCTIONS

Mouth is let ajar as an endless stream of voices rise through our throat and flood the room. Jaw locked in place. Tongue curling around chin. Eyes stretching open. We are immobile on the unlit stage.

In the end, these voices will lose their mobility. They will crowd and coagulate. Deteriorating as half-formed things. The skull dissolves.

SMUT

MAKER

SMUT

MAKER

ACT 1

"Three boys"

. . .

"I can see every absence now"

. . .

"there is too much"

. . .

"it is in his nature"

. . .

"radio signals ricocheting from wire to wire"

. . .

"what is the difference?"

. . .

"there are too many"

. . .

"he vomits"

. . .

"a sourceless scream"

. . .

"I don't know what you're getting at"

"a good rock is wide and flat"

. . .

. . .

"they?"

. . .

"they skip rocks on the lake"

. . .

"the overproduction of meaning"

. . .

"if he vomits then I will too"

. . .

"he doesn't know which to latch onto"

. . .

"behind us is the same car I saw on 94 earlier"

. . .

"can he speak?"

. . .

(applause)

"I

tendrils

"difference and differanc

. . .

"too many meanings"

. . .

"th

. .

"the word a projectile"

. . .

"he might be a real bastard"

. . .

"there is too much here"

. . .

"dense with fat"

. . .

"it was here before"

. . .

"in my dreams"

. . .

"if he does then I will too"

. . .

"I don't know the driver"

. . .

"her children are bulbous"

. . .

"made to be fried not to boiled"

. . .

"they were here before"

. . .

many
pread"

. . .

"who wrote the Wittgenstein?"

. . .

"I don't know what to grab onto."

"intentional miscommunications"

. . .

"teenagers loitering outside of Antwerp"

. . .

"he's left home to come here"

. . .

"too few interpretations"

. . .

"morphemes drip from his mouth"

. . .

"they are not properly projected"

. . .

"there is too much"

. . .

eing of all being"

"there is too much here"

. . .

"boy can speak but not speak well"

. . .

ACT 2

"no dreams"
. . .

"Blondboy alone in the apartment"
. . .

"I've cut myself on this door so many times"
. . .

"not here but near here"
. . .

(applause)

"stigmata open palm"
. . .

"two officers talk over their notes on the car crash"
. . .

"someone mentions a mugging"
. . .

"someone knocks on my door"
. . .

"reveal what is intimate"
. . .

"which have begun to levitate"
. . .

"they kiss and fuck"
. . .

"full of meaning"
. . .

"everything is simple"
. . .

"when the ashtray is full Blondboy leaves"
. . .

"blood aerated in my hands"
. . .

"sweet Blondboy sings every psalm he knows"
. . .

"a pattern of traffic cones"
. . .

"they don't do anything"
. . .

"new orifices breathing through fabric"
. . .

"like a fool"
. . .

"sways a light in front of his eyes"
. . .

"I know someone around here"
. . .

"Blondboy who lives around here"
. . .

"my mother moved here when I was young"
. . .

"somewhere that is cosmopolitan"
. . .

"blood or iron"
. . .

"blood concealed under bandaging"
. . .

"checks the back of his mouth"
. . .

"the doctor inspects the inside of his ear"
. . .

"strar corrects t sentim to a serie muggir

"Blondboy walks into my apartment"
. . .

"bodies mangled and unrecognizable"
. . .

(fade)

"burrowing into the rafters"
. . .

"the crashed cars are photographed and towed"
. . .

"carried onto the ceiling"
. . .

"any dreams tonight?"
. . .

"Blondboy strips down to his underwear and lies on the bed"
. . .

"distinguishing between who is automation and who is biological"
. . .

"everything is clear as day"
. . .

"the wall is covered in bent nails"
. . .

"arranged into an impossible architecture"
. . .

"from A and B to AB"
. . .

"I've been told"
. . .

"just fucking snatched"
. . .

"my dreams are made of copper and taste like iron or blood"
. . .

"when Blondboy is done they smoke cigarettes"
. . .

"I can't imagine that any of these arrows point towards something meaningful"
. . .

"nervous and stumbling"
. . .

"one thing leads to another"
. . .

"cars crash together outside"
. . .

"blood or iron"
. . .

"in search of lost meanings"
. . .

"I do not know where they went."

"no dreams tonight"
. . .

"bodies in uncanny positions"
. . .

"writes garbage erotica"
. . .

"who is built with robust materials and who is built with flesh"
. . .

"I cut open the flesh"
. . .

"when they are done smoking they go back inside"
. . .

"Mike Corrao writes his first harlequin novel"
. . .

"pedestrians left morbidly curious"
. . .

"He enters the wrong apartment"
. . .

"we live in a city"
. . .

"my son's watch was stolen right off his wrist"
. . .

"Blondboy again taking off his underwear and smiling"
. . .

"not here but near here"
. . .

"everything is simple"
. . .

"one of them lies on top of the other"
. . .

"two men lean against the balcony railing"
. . .

ACT 3

"Blondboy kissing his wrist and massaging his forearm"

. . .

"separating the muscle fibres with his thumbs"

. . .

"the first harlequin novel is smut"

. . .

"existentially speaking I think I've lost my appetite"

. . .

"if this is a new development"

. . .

"it haunts me"

. . .

"this is not a dream"

. . .

"it is a compulsion"

. . .

"if I have to go somewhere then it might as well be your place"

. . .

"where is Blondboy?"

. . .

"or if I'm just now realizing it"

. . .

"he comes over and they resume"

. . .

"then he's gone"

. . .

"where did they go?"

. . .

"I don't know if I ever had dreams"

. . .

(vomit)

"his face is ex

. .

"his offspri
set of trash
stacked int
snow man"

. . .

"I'm d

"Mike Corrao

"everything is dog shit"

. . .

"there
difference
erotic an

. .

"from the balcony"

. . .

"the doctor says there is nothing wrong"

. . .

"do not elevate him"

. . .

"when I close my eyes the televisior

ssionless"
"they pull the duvet off of the bed"
. . .
ke Corrao is
t" dog shit"
. . .
t write erotically"
"Eat the text"
. . .
ween
nut"
et to static."
(applause)
"now I feel like someone else's shit"
. . .
"left on the sidewalk for strangers to avoid"
. . .
"everything is simple"
. . .

"a television playing through an open window"

"I hear unfamiliar noises"
. . .

. . .
"not like you but faintly reminiscent"
. . .

"it's only a compulsion right now."

"khh bzz"
. . .

"or that it's source is something mundane and unimportant"
. . .

"the night shifts under spectral veil"
. . .

"I don't know"
. . .

"it doesn't matter"
. . .

"where I become paranoid that the noise never happened"
. . .

"I feel the desire to wander"
. . .

"it is not cicada season"
. . .

"an insectoid static"
. . .

"then
nothing"
. . .

ACT 5

"I've been thinking about my own existence too much"
. . . "I wander through uptown"

"where he vomits on my sheets"
. . .

"he tells me not to look directly at the sun"
. . .

. . . "old men stubbing cigarettes"

"document circumstances and witnesses"
. . .

. . .
"it's been so long but I can remember"
. . .

"I knew the man who drew this but I cannot remember his name"
. . .

"I remember"
. . .

"memories resurfacing"
. . .
"a figure standing obscured in the periphery"
. . .
"everyone I've known"
. . .
"its thingness"
. . .
"I want to get to the core of the thing"
. . .
"teeth bending outward like fibres of moustache"
. . .
"but I remember"
. . .

i
"it i

"slow
leading
the be

"my dreams are gone somewhere else"
. . .

"sp
olf

"someone somew
is sick of these ta
ledges"
. . .

"I remember
. . .

"the pillows duvet mattress box spring bed frame"
. . .

"Blondboy ne
waiting agains
wall"
. . .

"noted o
cop's
notepad
. . .

"you turn twenty-one or you die"
. . .

"takes my sheets to the laundromat"
. . .

"one thing or not at all"
. . .

"someone compressed against the ground"
. . .

"Blondboy looking out the window"
. . .

"an old man by now"
. . .

(black)

"image of arrows c

"apologizing so
about nerves o
. . .

"who can be special when they're a boy?"
. . .

"cycle running on laundry machine"
. . .

"him waiting in the hallway outside of my apartment"
. . .

"not how old I am"
. . .

"no one is ever sure what they're looking at"
. . .

"twenty-one years old"
. . .

"collision and mangled bodies"
. . .

"notes on a pad of paper"
. . .

"staining everything in a shade of yellow brown orange"
. . .

"but I remember"
. . .

"the wall of collected faces"
. . .

"a cop standing in front of the scene of the car crash"
. . .

"wher
remer
. . .

"mouth ajar"
. . .

"this does not mean anything"
. . .

(black)

vaded by an
rent meaning"
. . .

ble"

Blondboy throws
p on my bed
gain"
. . .

"vomit is the byproduct of nerves or diet"
. . .

g
"

orth of
twerp"
. . .

y

odors running in yellow brown orange hues"
. . .

nd one another in unfocused loops"
. . .

"he left in the morning"
. . .

"when I can remember to I think about nothing"
. . .

"everyone ends up the old boy"
. . .

"invaded by an emptiness."

"I've stopped the word boy"
. . .

"thudding my hip against walls and trash cans"
. . .

"waits next door"
. . .

"unfamiliar hands lead me to the precipice of a scaffolded structure"
. . .

"line along road surrounded by traffic cones"
. . .

"pupils dilated by the eye doctor"
. . .

"cops taking notes"
. . .

"of christ-like postures and the temptation"
. . .

"Blondboy lighting a cigarette and leaning against the wall"
. . .

"it is important to take notes at a crime scene so that you might later interpret what you are looking at"
. . .

"notes on notepad"
. . .

"we all need glasses"
. . .

"no more boys"
. . .

"blood on the ground"
. . .

"Blondboy parks in the lot of the apartment building"
. . .

"in a graveyard"
. . .

"it is important not to trust witnesses"
. . .

"everything turns out to be so simple"
. . .

"Oldboy"
. . .

"linens changing color as they are subjected to new hues"
. . .

"drawing arrows as they turn in on themselves"
. . .

"digging up bodies and putting them back"
. . .

ping on the floor"
. . .

"Blondboy on my bed"
. . .

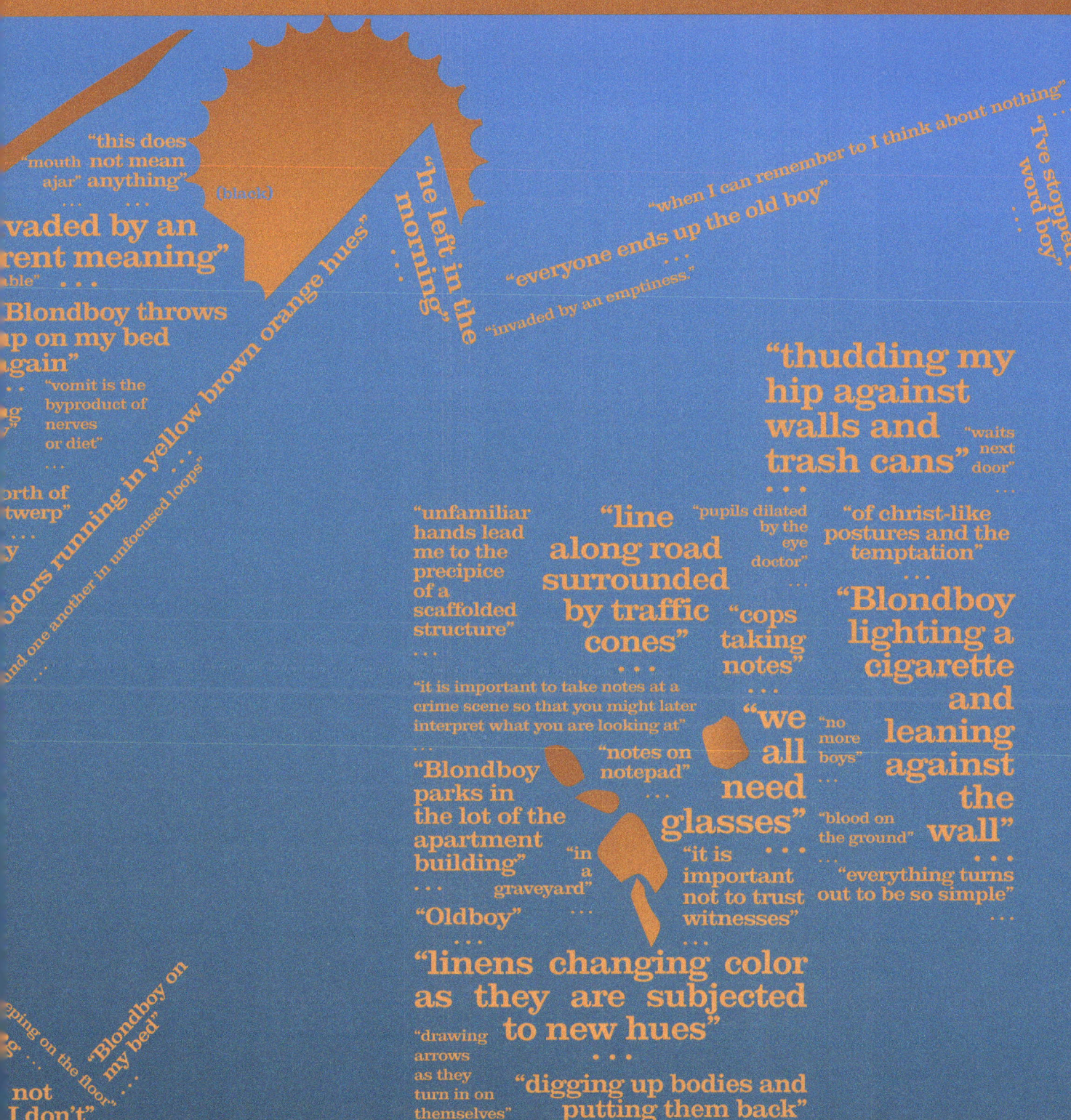

g"
not
I don't"

ACT 6

"linens running through the machine" . . . "coughing into his sleeve" . . .

"until the machine no longer wants to clean them" . . .

"I wander through a city dragging my feet over porous ground" . . .

"Blondboy sleeping on the floor again only to wake up next to me on the bed" . . .

"in search of lost meanings" . . .

"with asymmetrical towers and short palaces" . . .

"whether it is real or not" . . .

"under a flood of quiet voices" . . .

"I see static when I open my eyes" . . .

"tha this . . .

"over and over aga

"and draped over frames or radiat . . .

"passing cars" . . .

"what is the word for it?" . . .

"I can hear them now" . . .

"and still nothing" . . .

"Blondboy stubbing a cigarette into the sink" . . .

"and there is nothing worth mentioning" . . .

"like a mechanical reaction" . . .

"You never did the Kenosha Kid" . . .

"the screen reflecting static into his eyes" . . .

"A note arrives that says" . . .

"unplugging the television and plugging it back in" . . .

"hunger pains" . . .

"eyes turning red and opening the balcony door" . . .

"I can hear it all."

"and the last month" . . .

"without thought" . . .

"injections pressed into my elbow pit" . . .

"tall bastard squeezing his knuckles until the fat rolls out" . . .

omeone built
ief"

"it is easy to forget how intentional this image is"
. . .

"and I attempt to retrace my steps from the last week"
. . .

ntil they form to the grooves
s chamber"
. . .

"minute variations
in a terminal
architecture"
. . .

"waking up in
the laundromat
and praying to
the machine"
. . .

"and we start
etting them dry on the railing outside"
. . .

"responding only to the signified"
. . .

"there is no reason to ask"
. . .

"skyline draped across the
horizon"
. . .

"with the hope
of revitalizing
its desire to fix
your mistakes"
. . .

"cop
squatting
next to the
evidence"
. . .

"the materials of
its construction
pooling
together"
. . .

"he hears
violent
sounds
approaching"
. . .

"white noise accelerating towards a
deafening volume"
. . .

"mishaps
in the
usual
places"
. . .

"the
sun
changing
color"
. . .

"a dream coming to the surface"
. . .

(vomit)

ACT 7

"Blondboy offhandedly saying something about laundromats and coffee prices."

"Blondboy prioritizes himself"

"echoing tunnels"

"the compulsion to steer reckless"

. . .

"Sophie Calle following parisian men through Venice"

. . .

"Do you remember who came along to steal your hat?"

. . .

"coarse palm running over ribs"

. . .

"reflecting on office glass"

. . .

"in search of lost meanings"

. . .

"someone brings up narrator-fool Mike Corrao but quickly forgets why"

. . .

"all of the tenements woke at once"

. . .

"tall and lean"

. . .

"becoming-mason becoming-carpenter becoming-glassblower"

. . .

"sun coming over the skyline horizon"

. . .

"it must be one of them"

. . .

"so-s"

. . .

"no more filler"

. . .

"a suspect languishing over semiotic phantoms"

"there is . . . a list of culprits"

. . .

"no more descriptions"

. . .

(vomit)

"Blondboy stood outside of the laundromat with a cigarette in his mouth"

. . .

"hovering thumb over nipple"

. . .

"no ums"

. . .

"then standing outside of the laundromat again"

. . .

"calling a list of suspect phone numbers and investigating their source"

. . .

"it is not an altar"

. . .

"bleached hair short and combed back"

. . .

"the desperate need for something tangible"

. . .

"another attempt at sex"

. . .

"a physical object with its own individual aura"

. . .

"mound of bedsheets in his arms"

. . .

"fat knuckles"

. . .

"reading something at the kitchen table"

. . .

"the desire to make something that can be held onto"

. . .

"car crash shifting from horror to fantasy"

. . .

"uhs"

. . .

"light reflecting off of his bleached hair"

. . .

"grooves to displace the hand"

. . .

"I watched a photographer take photos of a young man"

. . .

"surgical rem

"na

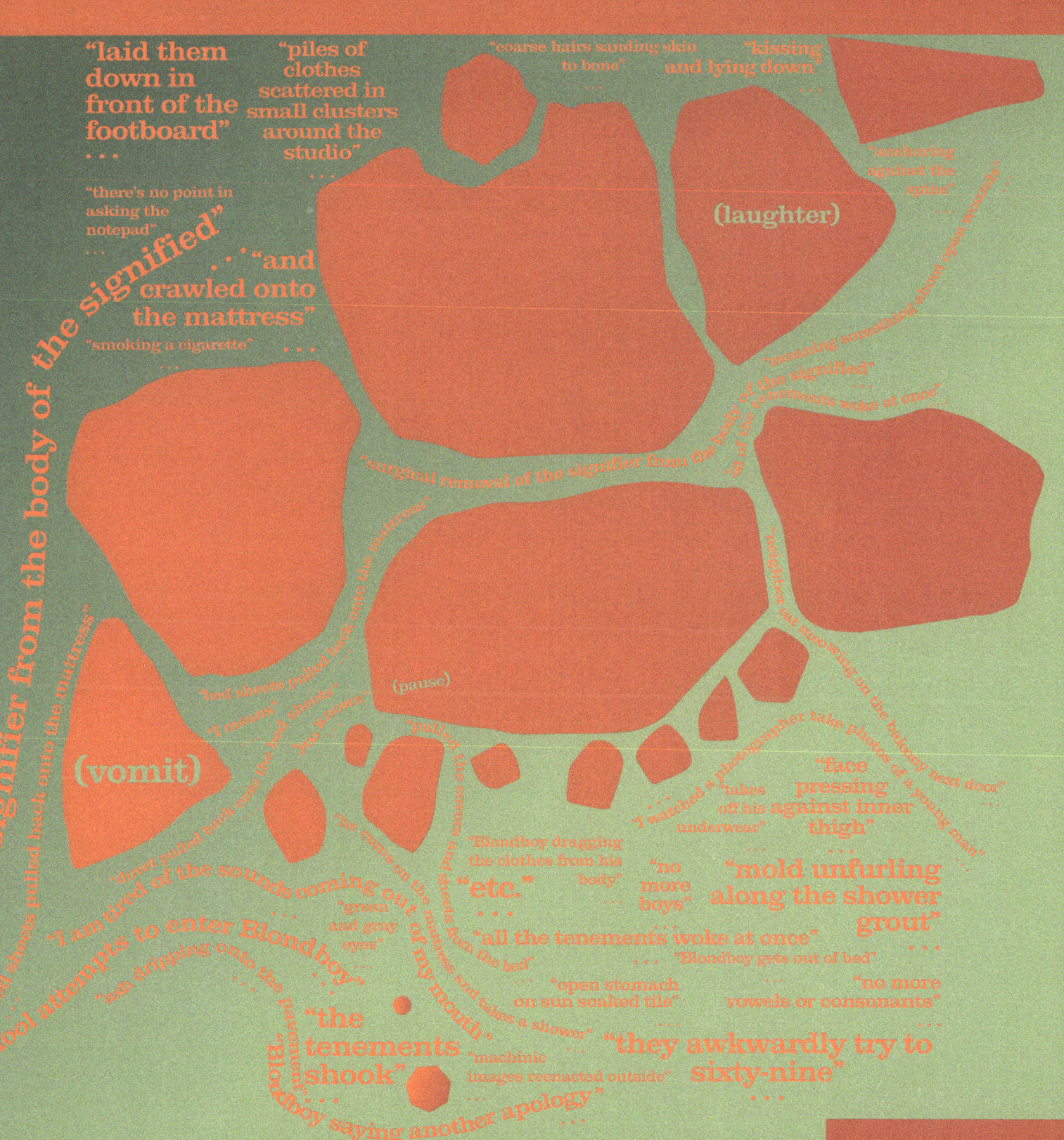

“laid them down in front of the footboard”
. . .

“piles of clothes scattered in small clusters around the studio”
. . .

“coarse hairs sanding skin to bone”
. . .

“kissing and lying down”
. . .

“there’s no point in asking the notepad”
. . .

signifier from the body of the signified”

. . . “and crawled onto the mattress”
. . .

“smoking a cigarette”
. . .

(laughter)

“anchoring against the spine”
. . .

“moaning something about open wounds”
. . .

“surgical removal of the signifier from the body of the signified”
. . .

“all of the tenements woke at once”
. . .

“bed sheets pulled back onto the mattress”
. . .

“bed sheets pulled back onto the mattress”
. . .

“I means”
. . .

“duvet pulled back onto the bed sheets”
. . .

“you knows”
. . .

(pause)

(vomit)

“neighbor cat meowing on the balcony next door”
. . .

“pulled the covers and sheets from the bed”
. . .

“he cums on the mattress and takes a shower”
. . .

“I watched a photographer take photos of a young man”
. . .

“takes off his underwear”
. . .

“face pressing against inner thigh”
. . .

“I am tired of the sounds coming out of my mouth”
. . .

“fool attempts to enter Blondboy”
. . .

“ash dripping onto the pavement”
. . .

“green and gray eyes”
. . .

“Blondboy dragging the clothes from his body”
. . .

“etc.”
. . .

“no more boys”
. . .

“mold unfurling along the shower grout”
. . .

“all the tenements woke at once”
. . .

“Blondboy gets out of bed”
. . .

“open stomach on sun soaked tile”
. . .

“no more vowels or consonants”
. . .

“the tenements shook”
. . .

“machinic images reenacted outside”
. . .

“they awkwardly try to sixty-nine”
. . .

“Blondboy saying another apology”
. . .

ACT 8

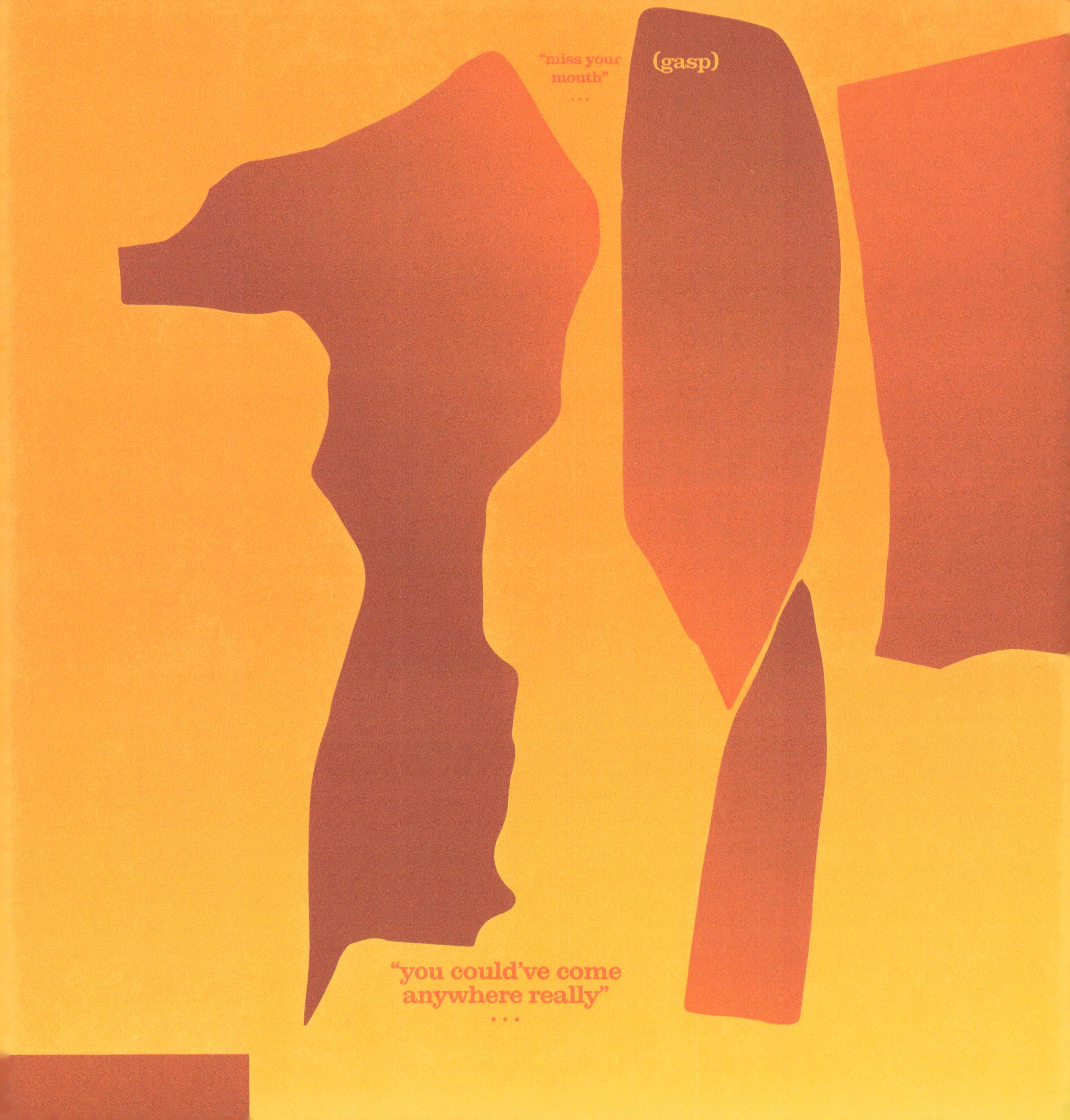
"miss your mouth" . . .
(gasp)
"you could've come anywhere really" . . .

"Narrator-fool Mike Corrao attempts to separate what is erotic from what is smut"
. . .

"unrolling like celluloid"
. . .

"with or without mound of sheets"
. . .

"stale patch left behind on mattress"
. . .

"in search of lost meanings"
. . .

"a stranger mutters something about the sterile generation"
. . .

"says that his mouth is filled with gravel"
. . .

"pluck it off the branch and pretend to take a bite"
. . .

"his tongue is made for uttering smut"
. . .

"a general suspicion"
. . .

"throw it behind your shoulder"
. . .

"trucks rocking under his window"
. . .

"there's no differance"
. . .

"I was in on every close call"
. . .

"no births no deaths no duration"
. . .

"Blondboy hesitant to feel like he accomplished something"
. . .

"try grabbing one"
. . .

"to tell what will make their task more satisfying"
. . .

"Blondboy tricked by psychogeography to stand outside and smoke a cigarette"
. . .

"no one's fucked since '92"
. . .

"laundromat assessing each machine"
. . .

"nobody can tell the difference"
. . .

"praying in front of their circular window"
. . .

"never met a twenty-four year old in my life"
. . .

"only ever twenty-fives and twenty-threes"
. . .

"asking each to reveal their desires"
. . .

"no one notices the differance"
. . .

"between one signifier and another."

"wouldn't have made a kid anyways"
. . .

"where have all these kids come from?"
. . .

ACT 9

"tea and coffee brewing"

. . .

"I didn't know they sold tea here"

. . .

"all of the tenements woke up at once"

. . .

"that's not true"

. . .

"every Chinese restaurant sells tea"

. . .

"digestions individual in their speed"

"synchronized movements and consumptions"

. . .

. . . "television humming static images."

"every place that you go that puts tea on your table is willing to sell you the leaves"

. . .

"that can't be true either"

. . .

"iced tea is tea but not really"

. . .

"every restaurant sells tea"

. . .

"a well-organized cityscape"

. . .

"in which this mass structure can be arranged by patterns of sleep"

. . .

"no sounds no disturbances"

. . .

ACT 10

"a bookstore that looks like a library"

. . .

"a department store that looks like an office building"

. . .

"a theater that looks like a warehouse"

. . .

"a grocery store that looks like an office building"

. . .

"a bar that looks like a bookstore"

. . .

"a department store that looks like a temple to money"

. . .

"a library that looks like a bookstore"

. . .

"a bank that looks like a bank"

. . .

"a bank that looks like a department store"

. . .

"a church that looks like a temple to money."

"An office building that looks like a bank"

. . .

"a library that looks like an office building"

. . .

"a department store that looks like a library"

. . .

"an office building that looks like a grocery store"

. . .

"a bar that looks like a library"

. . .

"a grocery store that looks like a bank"

. . .

"a bank that looks like a library"

. . .

"a pub that looks like an office building"

. . .

"a department store that looks like a grocery store"

. . .

"a bar that looks like a library"

. . .

"a pub that looks like a bar"

. . .

"a cafe that looks like a pub"

. . .

"a library that looks like a bar"

. . .

"a pub that looks like a bank"

. . .

"a bank that looks like a department store"

. . .

"a bank that looks like temple to money"
. . .

"a warehouse that looks like a theater"
. . .

"a bank that looks like a warehouse"
. . .

"a library that looks like a warehouse"
. . .

"a bank that looks like a library"
. . .

"a library that looks like a bookstore"
. . .

"a cafe that looks like a deli"
. . .

"a pub that looks like an office building"
. . .

"a bar that looks like a grocery store"
. . .

"a theater that looks like a warehouse"
. . .

"a cafe that looks like a library"
. . .

"a grocery store that looks like a theater"
. . .

"a department store that looks like a bar"
. . .

"a pub that looks like an office building"
. . .

"a grocery store that looks like a deli"
. . .

"an office building that looks like a warehouse"
. . .

"an office building that looks like a bank"
. . .

"a bar that looks like a cafe"
. . .

"a deli that looks like a pub"
. . .

"a bank that looks like an office building"
. . .

ACT 11

"Blondboy made his bed in the apartment"
...

"untranscribed documents catalogued in intentionally obtuse locations"
...

"Blondboy sitting alone on the washing machine"
...

"took a shower and sat on the balcony"
...

"tools for sifting through white noise"
...

"adjacent to the sun-bathing neighbor cat"
...

"temporary solutions to a larger problem"
...

"my mouth the source of unnecessary dialogues"
...

"v2 rockets will collide in the upper atmosphere or the planet will remain still for a hundred years"
...

"tenants and landlord and passersby"
...

"everything's been replaced by static"
...

"a plastic reenactment of the ballardian crash fantasy"
...

"talk of old cops and messages from north of Antwerp"
...

"natural eyes removed and replaced with the kino"
...

"misleading notepads and missing campers"
...

"all of the tap water has been poisoned"
...

"it is not good to spend your time with confident people"
...

"smut-maker lies sick in bed for three days"
...

"towers of static"
...

"in which machines are entangled with his body"
...

"thinking about certain radio signals"
...

"smut-maker debates migrating deeper into the cityscape."

"if he comes around again scream in his mouth"
...

"nothing will happen or too much will happen"
...

(applause)

"Blondboy smokes another cigarette outs of the laundromat"
...

"looking back at the thudding machinery and tunneling linens"
...

"in a blasé state"
...

and throws up in

"everyone's a pas
...

"carved in arcane shapes"
...

"Blondboy squats on the sidewalk outside and eats a sandwich"
...

"he pulls the skin from his chin and neck"
...

"dream thief"
...

"fantasies of other people"
...

"wandering through nighttime cityscape"
...

"the non-descript uptown scenery"
...

"subsists off of the found or purchased nutrients"
...

"j t a si

"dar opa

"dri paper cof

"fuck Blond and le
...

"in search

of cardboard and styrofoam"

. . .

"people move around him"

. . .

"waiting"

. . .

"Blondboy fucks the
nut-maker
oilet after"

. . .

"exposing his gums to the open air"

. . .

by"

"cold and ever-changing"

. . .

"foreign documents rising through a column of smoke"

. . .

"large blotches of static"

. . .

"hallucinatory alleyways"

. . .

"occupied by something phantasmagoric"

. . .

"and he does not feel fear"

. . .

"curved mien of the narrator-fool"

. . .

"the sun changes hues"

. . .

"in a time when there are too many meanings"

. . .

"the rhizomatic labyrinth of mirrored buildings"

. . .

"something about cocks and ropes"

. . .

"laughing at his own idiotic joke"

. . .

"experiences his only dream"

. . .

"unknown creatures tearing away slabs of cardboard"

. . .

"purpose rendered into bricabrac"

. . .

"and you never learned how to sex someone with a clear head"

. . .

"the year of all reason"

. . .

"building small pyramids over the grates of storm drains"

. . .

"minerals oozing through fractures in the metal piping"

. . .

"obfuscated mise-en-scene"

. . .

"prettier and larger than myself"

. . .

"tell him to go"

. . .

st meaning"

"everybody is waiting"

. . .

"Blondboy filters his water through coffee"

. . .

"I want my head to explode"

. . .

ACT 12

"End of acts one through twelve"

. . .

"the dissipation of the first stream of voices"

. . .

"where my mouth has become incredibly tired"

(applause)

(black and laughter)

. . .

"for somewhere entirely unrecognizable"

. . .

"you're pulled over the horizon by the strong arm of helios"

. . .

"departing with the sun"

. . .

"and my audience has left"

. . .

"you're pulled over the horizon by the str

arm of helios”

ACT 13

"Smut-maker under the guise of a fool narrator"
. . .
"vomiting lines from Proust"
. . .
"tongue slithering through ear canal"
. . .
"thoughts rising"
. . .
"golem of dripping cataplasm moaning from its trash mouth"
. . .
"s
th

"in search of lost meaning"
. . .
"memories rising"
. . .
"a set of books that he has not read"
. . .
"old policemen"
. . .
"talk about their taxes"
. . .
"two men with separat
personalities
talk with one
another"
. . .

"and that he does not have any desire to read"
. . .
"the unidentifiable offspring that they have been paid to build"
. . .
"limb to text"
. . .
"lip pulling away from gums"
. . .
"their personalities remain incompatible"
. . .
"an order of dreams and memories"
. . .
"Blondboy enters dream and sits on the edge of bed"
. . .
"you do not kno
are spelling it t
with their voice
. . .

"differences and differances"
. . .
"shift from past to present"
. . .
"things that are taxing"
. . .
"mounds of trash and debris"
. . .
in

"lying across the circumference of his waist"
. . .
"laborer inspecting their labor"
. . .
"new identities come together and coagulate on the floor"
. . .
"resurrected poet dressed in an ashen frame"
. . .
"with inescapable width"
. . .
"someone r
. . .

"neighbor cat with stomach pressed against cool tile"
. . .
"Blondboy shitting with the door open"
. . .
"smut-maker on bus and sidewalk"
. . .
"him"
. . .
"wall of flesh collecting new materials for its fragile construction"
. . .
"I've take
somethin
from you
. . .

"several attempts to light the filter of a cigarette"
. . .
"Henry and Veronica saying something about a minotaure"
. . .
"Mike Corrao sees Roberto Bolaño on the bus"
. . .
"it's not wh
were trying

"bodies amassing into a wall of orgies"
. . .
"no more boys"
. . .
"knees compressing against diorite steps"
. . .
"live television audience with back hunched over plastic mise-en-scene"
. . .
"assembly line churning"
. . .
"you say that you don't want this"
. . .
"Bolaño
away an
. . .

"maenads weaving through the gaps"
. . .
"I do not dream anymore"
. . .
"beast slouching into th
. . .
"Orpheus weeps on the steps of the underworld"
. . .
"towers of cardboard"
. . .
"apparitions dragging the dreams out of my skull"
. . .
"in a fog of linens"
. . .
"it will be there forever"
. . .
"maen
cr
into your mo
"all of my thoughts come true at once"
. . .

"my purpose comes from the symbols of another"
. . .
"I do not know where boys run off to"
. . .
"no more boys"
. . .
"my children will dream of colossal turquoise structures"
. . .
"drifting slowly into the air and caressing the ceiling"
. . .
"objects swelling with gas"
. . .
"vomit stained across ever
. . .

"it's lost on me now"
. . .
"sounds converging in a deafening crescendo"
. . .
"I do not want to hear it from someone else"
. . .
"life is nothing but a series of"
. . .
wh
be g
in
"brass instruments sing across the horizon"
. . .

said that
l time's
ı but I've
ıp every
ıe"

"the first harlequin novel arranged into dust-coated towers"

. . .

"begging for the mantis to behead him"

. . .

"I want to feel weightless"

. . .

"I want to witness a severing"

. . .

"photos of your previous stigmata"

. . .

"I remember how it starts and ends"

. . .

"I want to see it myself"

. . .

"I can see the way the day bends in on itself"

. . .

st, second, third,
rth, etc."

"cracks re-open on the road surface"

. . .

"Blondboy remembered all of his awkward sexual encounters"

. . .

"all of the skyscrapers feel as if they're bending in towards me"

. . .

"there is too much here now"

. . .

ıg in the
tub like
is de Sade"

. . .

"every person he tried to fuck"

. . .

"the bus locomotes"

. . .

"how the middle drifts in irregular fits"

. . .

"compresses his brow bone and break my hand"

hy they
vay

"the vomit on the comforter and the bed sheets"

. . .

"styrofoam fuels pitch-colored fires
ripheries of downtown"

. . .

"etc."

. . .

"coated in thin layers of asphalt"

. . .

"they look down at me with arcing spines"

. . .

"your actions are elliptical"

. . .

"curved into tunnels"

. . .

ıe to burn everything"

. . .

"I want to pull god's jaw from his skull"

. . .

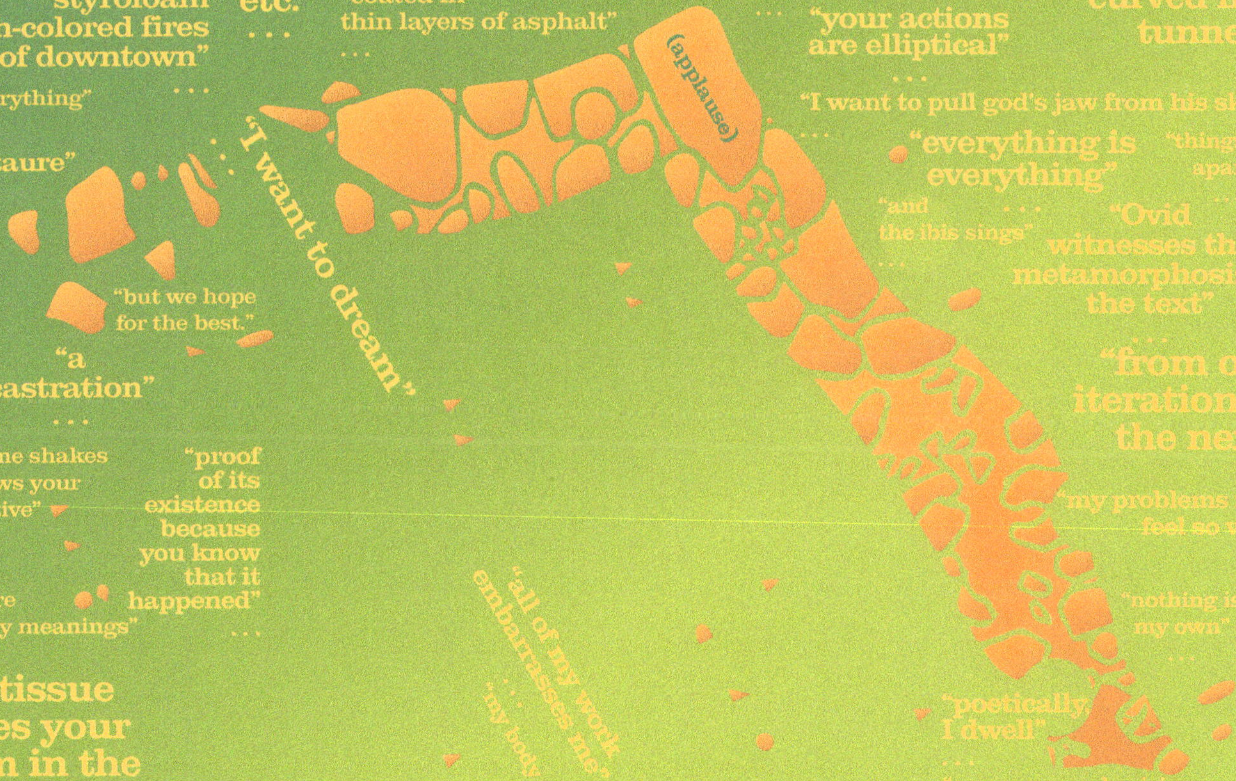

(applause)

"I want to dream"

ns a minotaure"

rovels on his
s and asks to
forgiven"

. . .

"everything is everything"

. . .

"things fall apart"

. . .

"and the ibis sings"

. . .

"Ovid witnesses the metamorphosis of the text"

. . .

"but we hope for the best."

veryone
eaves at
once"

. . .

"a castration"

. . .

"from one iteration to the next"

. . .

ou
ve
e"

. . .

"the frame shakes and skews your perspective"

. . .

"proof of its existence because you know that it happened"

. . .

"my problems now feel so vast"

. . .

imself
es"

"there are too many meanings"

. . .

"all of my work embarrasses me"

. . .

"my body swaying through uptown alone"

. . .

"nothing is my own"

. . .

"I wonder what is up north of Antwerp"

"scar tissue irritates your forearm in the hot and dry temperatures of the morning"

. . .

"poetically, I dwell"

. . .

"a young man bruising his tailbone"

. . .

"an old cop drinking oil from the pores of the cement"

. . .

"if there was anything clear to say"

. . .

surface"

"anomalous architectures"

. . .

"Blondboy enters a memory and spits mucous into the sink well"

. . .

ACT 14

"silhouettes gathering around the hearth"
. . .

"when the wall has collapsed someone asks if he wants to have coffee together"
. . .

"Maenads sex the wall of orgy bodies"
. . .

"nothing meaningful ever happens in a cafe"
. . .

"maenads build a shrine"
. . .

"whisper something about intentions"
. . .

"I feel possessed."

"the coffee is too hot and he burns his tongue"
. . .

"whisper something about the act of severing"
. . .

"pareidolic images emerging"
. . .

"there is nothing worth looking at"
. . .

"static looming at the same arc as the surface below"
. . .

"it's three o'clock and he's twenty-one like me"
. . .

"limbs lost in the destruction of the orgy wall"
. . .

"there is nothing here"
. . .

"when I enter the next room there is a wall of television black"
. . .

"I'll be twenty-seven like him"
. . .

"the black that is not black but a multitude of disparate colors"
. . .

"until there is no one left trudging through this shitty wasteland"

. . .

(applause)

"I found rats stacked in pyramids over the grates of storm drains"

. . .

(laughter)

"Narrator-fool remembers attempt to enter Blondboy"

. . .

(laughter)

"corpses taint the tap water with the formaldehyde from their veins"

. . .

(laughter)

"cloaked figures rearrange my organs as I sleep"

. . .

(laughter)

(laughter)

"I am without the desire to create new life"

. . .

(laughter)

(laughter)

(laughter)

"I am without children"

. . .

"radiator-man continues to haunt my family"

"my music mimics the sounds of a car crash"

. . .

(laughter)

(laughter)

(laughter)

"only the desire to perpetuate my own."

. . .

"my death will be witnessed and archived by CCTV cameras."

ACT 16

"Everything I see is formed from distant blotches of color"
. . .

"you live a life of vagueness"
. . .

"images made in the likeness of Seurat"
. . .

"where each stranger appears identical"
. . .

"expressions are unreadable"
. . .

"computational deities resurrecting old servers and siphoning the nutrients from their bodies"
. . .

"the shift from black to red to orange to yellow to white"
. . .

"I cannot remember"
. . .

"but I do not know what or where"
. . .

"my knees are sore and I do not want to try bending my back"
. . .

"my dictations will form a new landscape"
. . .

"everything feels as if it is being spelled wrong"
. . .

"subject walking through the non-descript cityscape"
. . .

"but I hope when you come back to me"
. . .

"smut is where everyone is satisfied"
. . .

"you will see it in the moment"
. . .

"pores excreting lubricant"
. . .

"nothing is nothing"
. . .

"faint sounds of lip against metal" . . .

"I lack information."

"sorting through the mass of data"
. . .

"crowd turning"
. . .

"there is too much now"
. . .

"walls bloating"
. . .

"one day they will resurrect the images that have rotted my vision"
. . .

"air is warm and dry"
. . .

"my memories are there but I cannot remember"
. . .

"a union of spot welders"
. . .

"circular muscle tightening around zone" . . .

"I will see them again when it comes time to revisit what has happened"

. . .

"mysterious substances coagulating around the base of the ceiling fan"

. . .

"every vein and bone traced onto the adjacent wall"

. . .

"sunlight is warm and dry"

. . .

"colors are warm and dry"

. . .

"there is nothing to see here"

. . .

"it is done with intention"

. . .

"hurry up please it's time to go"

. . .

"there is nothing left but the faint shouting of strangers outside"

. . .

"becoming the laminated film of a projector"

. . .

"skin becoming translucent in the light"

. . .

"machinic growths forming in the wall between the outside and inside"

. . .

"organism fed by its moist environment"

. . .

"street view turning"

. . .

"each organ its own rhizome"

. . .

"memory of Blondboy saying something about the labyrinth"

. . .

"stomach turning"

. . .

"a misspelling of minotaure"

. . .

"why is that there"

. . .

"that is not an answer"

. . .

"the grooves of the flesh turn in on themselves creating new patterns"

. . .

"I wander through uptown until the buildings stretch into downtown"

. . .

"I do not know where midtown is"

. . .

"there is a lull in activity"

. . .

"it is not between uptown and downtown"

. . .

"memory of Blondboy ritualistically pissing forked after sex"

. . .

"every pause in my speech a mark of the greater topography"

. . .

"the slow rise of humming"

. . .

"each encounter accelerating towards a form process"

. . .

"this is fucking boring"

. . .

"not too too much"

. . .

"along the face of inner thigh"

. . .

"altar made in the likeness of taint gods"

. . .

"montage of hips and outer thigh"

. . .

"there is something I should be looking for"

. . .

"somewhere that I am supposed to be going"

. . .

"or like the spelling has changed"

. . .

"each older version stored in an obscure archive"

. . .

"organized by opening morpheme"

. . .

"what are you accelerating towards?"

. . .

"trail of lube dripping behind"

. . .

"maenads slithering between arm and torso"

. . .

ACT 17

"Bolaño says that he ran off of the bus because our encounter was jarring and violent"

. . .

"smut-maker attempts to map his connection to another writer"

. . .

"when their work only overlaps o

. . .

"Blondboy refuses to change his t

. . .

"techniques involving small stones and torn cloth"

. . .

"someone says that they know how to manipulate time"

. . .

"in the tradition of Bergson's du

. . .

"no more boys"

. . .

"in the city I feel like a wastrel"

. . .

"moving without a place to move towards"

. . .

"converting a labor of progression labor of movement itself"

. . .

"the slow teeth of a Russian Stalker combing through the grass"

. . .

"news about a group of campers that went missing north of Antwerp"

. . .

"I've begun to separate from my skeleton"

. . .

"fibres snapping along each junction"

. . .

"feet treading over luminous soil"

. . .

"where I do not feel obligated to go somewhere"

. . .

"in the tradition of Schoonover"

. . .

"Blondboy remains Blondboy."

ACT 18

"I watch a series of city films"

. . .

"and note the movement of each subject"

. . .

"a city is made from bodies and architecture"

. . .

"reduce image down to two elements"

. . .

"lack in one area renders the space uncanny"

. . .

"ooooo."

"new dreams appear in my memory"

. . .

"rockets fire off in the middle of the night"

. . .

"I think the end is finally here"

. . .

ACT 19

"Have you read the Wittgenstein?"

. . . "falling between star and drifting debris"

"silhouette crashes down to Earth"

. . .

"Breton says something about his own psychogeographies"

"your actions are predictable"

. . .

. . .

"his skin coated in the ash of his impact"

. . .

"we are all similar people"

. . .

"Incipit plume of lavender colored smoke"

. . .

"crater forming in an open field"

. . .

"but the results are uninteresting and you quickly forget"

. . .

"aliens have been here since the beginning"

"pyramids built in the likeness of spaceships"

. . .

"we speak"

. . .

"lying dormant underground"

. . .

"Sun Ra praising the construction of an ark"

. . .

"it doesn't matter"

. . .

"if anybody arrived here from another planet"

. . .

"it is him"

. . .

"did you see the rockets firing last night?"

. . .

"loitering is a symptom of avant-gardists"

. . .

"I can see the signs now"

. . .

"a short and angry woman rubs the ash from his face and hands"

. . .

"there are reasonable people and unreasonable people"

. . .

"needless practice in reduction"

. . .

"you search for a new praxis"

. . .

"there are Bolaño's and smut-makers"

. . .

"I've met people from space"

. . .

"is there an event"

. . .

"respecting the shape of this new threshold"

"someone mentions Tommyboy"

"in order to fully appreciate this architecture you might have to fuck it"

. . .

. . .

"I can only trust my mother" . . .

"there is no differance"

. . .

. . .

"one signifier leading to another"

. . .

"they say to ask him where this nothingness has come from"

. . .

"I've been told that we're on Earth but I don't know what that implies"

. . .

"the walls remain dirty"

. . .

"he sits in my living room watching a visual album"

. . .

"physique of a cosmic anatomy"

. . .

"employees clean the windows and floors"

. . .

"he and I"

. . .

"he refuses to speak and communicates through facial expressions instead"

. . .

"your gestures are symbo difficult to interpret"

. . .

"Tommyboy burns down a country of forests"

. . .

"no memories"

. . .

"people are woven from strings"

. . .

"the ash and evidence are cleaned from his body"

. . .

"he says he doesn't k where he is"

. . .

"what planet this is"

. . .

"no dreams"

. . .

"helios drags ear of lamb over the sunset"

. . .

"Tommyboy curls his body on the floor."

"in w gen are su to su muta

"reorg ther in t enviro

"cock slopin

"Mexican avant-gardists linger on the deck of a cafe"

. . .

"I do not know

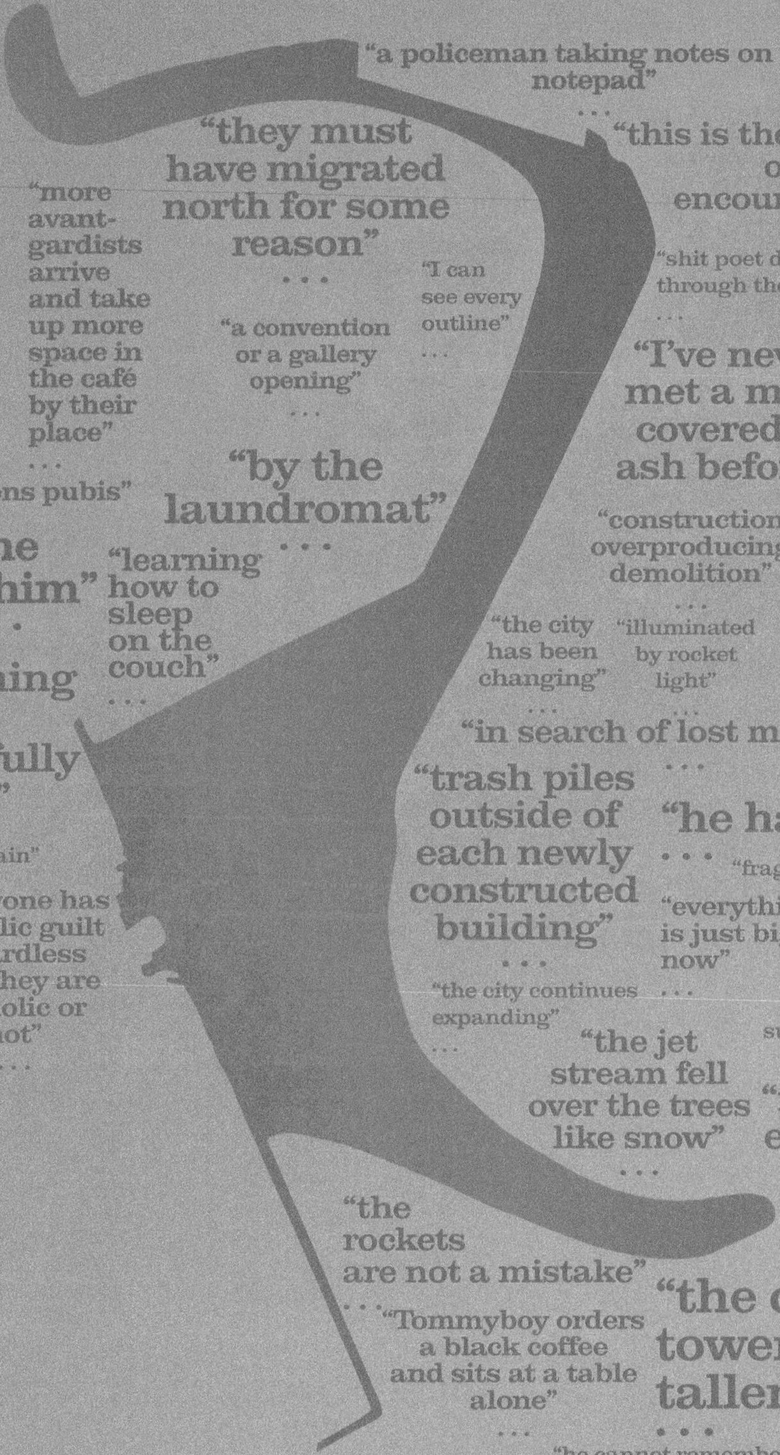

ch
ia
ct
en
n"
• • •
ng
res
ew
nt"
. . .
. mons pubis"

"me
d him"
• • •

aning
he
y fully
ns"

contain"

veryone has
tholic guilt
regardless
f if they are
catholic or
not"
. . .

"more
avant-
gardists
arrive
and take
up more
space in
the café
by their
place"
. . .

"a policeman taking notes on his
notepad"
. . .

"they must
have migrated
north for some
reason"
• • •

"I can
see every
outline"
. . .

"a convention
or a gallery
opening"
. . .

"by the
laundromat"
• • •

"learning
how to
sleep
on the
couch"
. . .

"I was not the
only witness"
. . .

"metonym
dislodging itself
from the larger
image"
. . .

"this is the year
of new
encounters"
. . .

"as every
circumstance tends
to be"
. . .

"shit poet drifting his car
through the Sonora desert"
. . .

"but the
circumstances are
strange"
. . .

"a remark about the
expression of the
passenger"
. . .

"I've never
met a man
covered in
ash before"
. . .

"the doctor
says there isn't
any physical
ailment"
. . .

"they are
scared away
by the crash"
. . .

"construction
overproducing
demolition"
. . .

"in a world where
every doorway
appears yonic"
• • •

"every
new
essay
lies to
me"
. . .

"the city
has been
changing"
. . .

"illuminated
by rocket
light"
. . .

"in search of lost meaning"
. . .

"I don't know what it means"
. . .

"trash piles
outside of
each newly
constructed
building"
• • •

"he has a strange face"
• • •

"he says
that he is
okay"
. . .

"fragments will be made from metal and ash"
. . .

"everything
is just bigger
now"
. . .

"Tommyboy
mentions a dream
about two
surrealists and a chance
sexual encounter"
. . .

"there was no
concussion"
. . .

"the city continues
expanding"
. . .

"the jet
stream fell
over the trees
like snow"
. . .

"it has been
expanding"
. . .

"I don't
know the
ethics of our
interaction"
. . .

"we are acquainted now"
. . .

"the
rockets
are not a mistake"
. . .

"we share an apartment"
. . .

"he mouths
the words
that he would
like to speak
aloud"
. . .

"Tommyboy orders
a black coffee
and sits at a table
alone"
. . .

"the cardboard
towers have grown
taller"
• • •

"Tommyboy fell from space and I know this"
. . .

"he cannot remember what their names were
but they were both Spanish"
. . .

"a chain of metaphors
linking together"
. . .

ACT 20

"the sentiment of the minister is ugly" . . . "no one is speaking the same language" . . . "the doors are stripped from their hinges" . . . "each guest is offered a cigarette and a coffee" . . . "clusters of

"sex is a performance and he does not like this" . . .

"a motif permeates the ceremony" . . .

"A marriage is quickly prepared" . . .

"and each guest must press their fingernails against the page" . . .

"one of the newly arrived Mexican avant-gardists proposes an impromptu wedding" . . .

"he and Tommyboy bring a pot of coffee and a handmade registry" . . .

"but the moment feels right" . . .

"communication is done p

"someone genero leaves a well of b

"but there i no pen" . . .

"and for now it is good."

"T th

vall
orn
rom
me"
. . .

ens their hand and
sides the booklet" "parents are not
invited"
. . .

"no one is talking
t the same thing"
. . .

nyboy says
e can only
when he
turbates"
. . .

rily through hand gestures and facial expressions"
. . .

ACT 21

"ascends into the sky and quickly crash back onto the ground"

. . . "Sun Ra prays the construction of his ark"

"space is the place"

. . .

"he places cock of narrator-fool in mouth"

. . .

"Tommyboy continues to stay at my apartment"

. . .

"we think about fucking when we are alone"

. . .

"what are you accelerating towards?" . . .

. . .

"and at first we circumnavigate this idea"

. . .

"the sheets remain on the bed"

. . .

"who I did not know of"

. . .

"I can't see it"

. . .

"flattens his hand over my inner thigh and slowly inches towards it"

. . .

"but then we do not"

. . .

"placing his hand over and then pulling away" . . .

. . .

"people don't talk to each other directly"

. . .

"I do not mind this"

. . .

"they close their eyes during a lunch break and then return to work"

. . .

"du

"there is too much here now"

. . .

"no one ever sleeps"

. . .

"images of a yonic landscape"

. . .

"asks to be rewarded"

. . .

"and says that the narrator-fool should sleep on that pillow tonight."

"even though he is married to someone else"

. . .

“he sits ass to heels on the bed” . . .

“Tommyboy attempts to do something passionate” . . .

“legs spread open until the body is split in half” . . .

“rolls his tongue around its weight”

“too many meanings and implications” . . .

“I hear people through fragments of speech” . . .

“sex is a purely aesthetic activity” . . .

“no one trusts your government” . . .

“people have taken photographs before” . . .

“Tommyboy says that he is not sure and does not want to do anything that he might later regret” . . .

“completes on the pillow”

“and closes his eyes” . . .

“he crawls onto my body” . . .

“Tommyboy says something about only coming when he masturbates” . . .

“does not moan but breathes heavily” . . .

“and loses interest” . . .

“forming across a desert” . . .

ACT 22

"so that whatever keratin has been lost can be reintroduced"
. . .

"although I have difficulty recognizing this difference as well"
. . .

"I think that it is related to the difference between writing and construction"
. . .

"obelisks are carved from recycled columns"
. . .

"I do not know what creates the distinction between avant-gardist and regular poet"
. . .

"cordyceps slowly expanding in the empty space of the skull"
. . .

"Tommyboy and Blondboy are connected through the people they have fucked"
. . .

"I want my dreams to invade the daytime"
. . .

"if the rocket hits them then it will bounce off of the edge and fly somewhere else"
. . .

"fingernails peared into crescents"

"the city continues to expand"
. . .

"I know three of the Mexic
avant-gardists wh
say they would clas
themselves as poe
. . .

"sun changing hues"
. . .

"blue yell
orange wh
. . .

"the pyramids are a safe place"
. . .

"nonsense can be therapeutic"
. . .

"OOOOO"
. . .

myboy
npts
eak in
y"

"he tries
to say
that he's
chosen to
live here
because
it is
chaotic
and livid"
. . .

"the
organism
an
ecosystem"
. . .

"they are good in their own
right"

"converting
text into a
semantic
geometry"
. . .

"doom . . .
is not
impending"
. . .

"I've never read the
Wittgenstein"
. . .

"drummer percusses baton
against flat face"
. . .

"my body demands sleep"
. . .

"they are
consumed
for their
nutrients"
. . .

"I ask about the
avant-gardist and
their marriage"
. . .

"field of porous
stones and moss
film"
. . .

"sound
of brass
flooding
a narrow
alleyway"
. . .

"in the tradition
of Deleuze's
something"
. . .

"I cannot remember"
. . .

"my experience here has
become immanent"
. . .

"and render
me mobile."

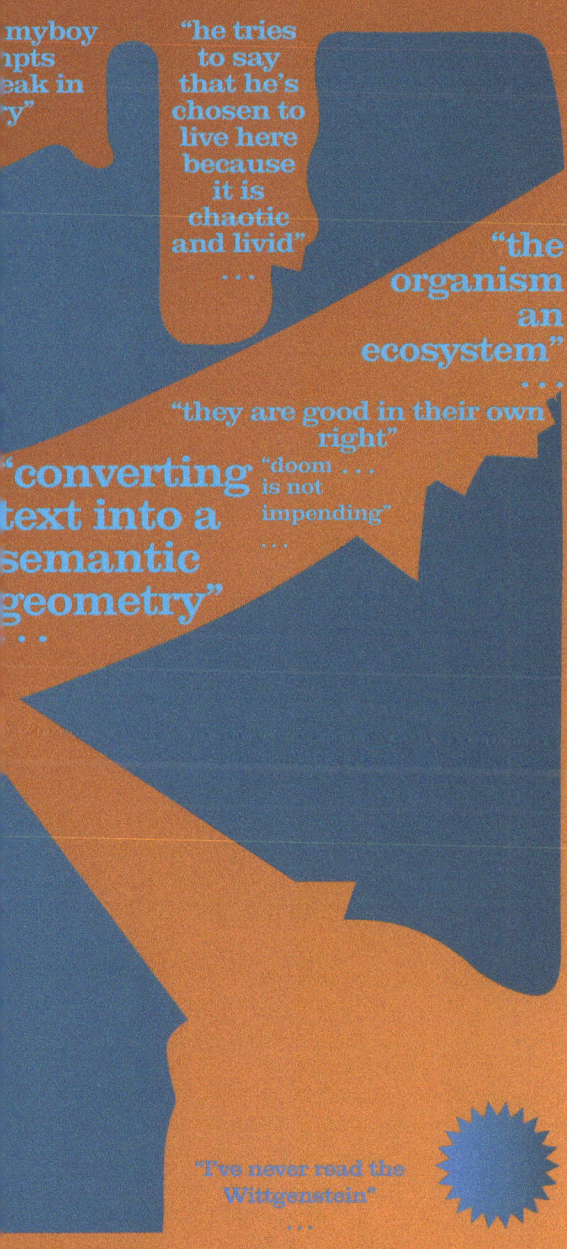

ACT 23

"or that does not have any reason to exist"
. . .

"each match is lit individually"
. . .

"or meani
that has ye
reveal itsel
. . .

"an eye exam says that you can only see what you want to see"
. . .

"Tommyboy remains Tommyboy"
. . .

"my mouth the source of this sound"
. . .

"where older sounds have begun to rise to the surface"
. . .

"my throat the archive of other beings"
. . .

"I feel like I
been talking a
him too m

"that my voice ha
become too unifie
. . .

has tra
in

"and begun
down m

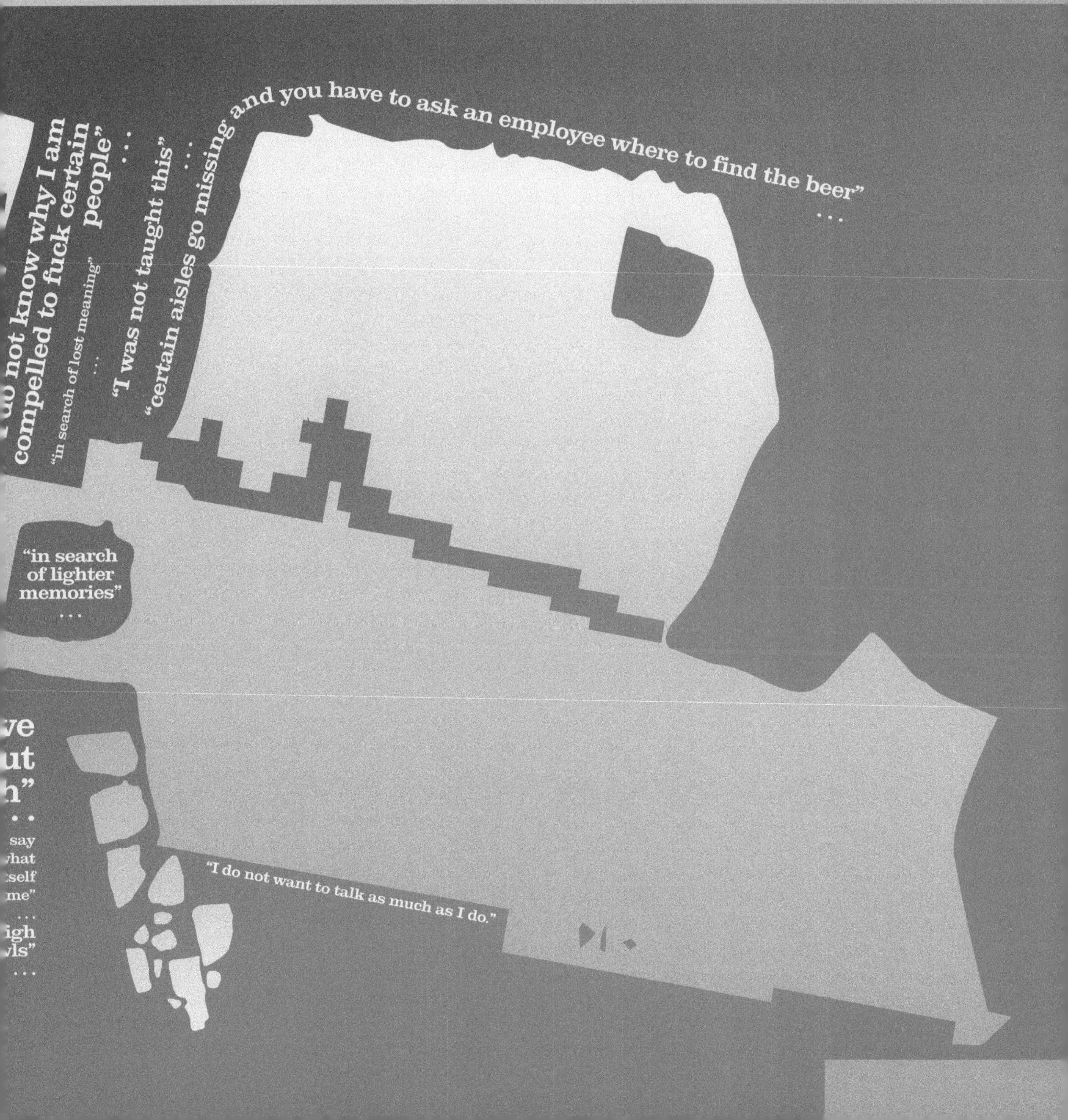
do not know why I am
compelled to fuck certain
people"
. . .
"in search of lost meaning"
. . .
"I was not taught this"
. . .
"certain aisles go missing and you have to ask an employee where to find the beer"
. . .
"in search
of lighter
memories"
. . .
ve
ut
n"
. .
say
hat
self
me"
. . .
igh
vls"
. . .
"I do not want to talk as much as I do."

ACT 24

"I am told there are no hospitals in the vacuum of space"

. . .

"I return to consciousness"

. . .

"I feel possessed"

. . .

"collidi

. . .

"Tommybo

"my
is dis
its co

. . . "

(laughter).

the dishes and sleeps on
e couch" . . .

"doctor noting on notepad"

"unknown mancer casting body
horrors onto my self" . . .

nbled and . . .
nents are recycled"

"everything is
so loud" . . .

"Barthes
reorienting a large
mechanism" . . .

ing weekends he
eps on the beds"

"when
I go to
sleep" . . .

"old cop . . .
quats next
to a car
crash" . . .

"all of the tenements
woke at once"

"but these afflictions do not last
long" . . .

"a creature of habit" . . .

"it is
meaningless
otherwise" . . .

"my head
swelling
with
occult
materials" . . .

"every thought coagulating together
in a mess of tissue" . . .

"subjects
float like
asteroids" . . .

"faux novelist
drinking his own
piss" . . .

"subways
looped into
a mobius
strip" . . .

"flesh and
flavor of a
grapefruit" . . .

"we must simply arrive" . . .

"wizard
of gore" . . .

"my arrival on this
planet was bitter" . . .

"an alley . . . of larches" . . .

o absorb this moment all at once" . . .

"memories
resurfacing" . . .

"there cannot be a
progression" . . .

"curled into the fetal position" . . .

"I can hear when the white noise
disappears" . . .

"I am possessed by
languored towers of steam" . . .

ACT 25

"the key to falling is to lengthen your slowing down"

. . .

"narrator-fool chokes on hot coffee"

. . .

"you look for the distinction between semiotics and syntax"

. . .

"an apparition taking the shape of something I am only unconsciously familiar with"

. . .

"the collision of two celestial bodies is a controlled phenomenon"

. . .

"it begins with the way that you move your tongue"

. . .

"smut-maker attempts a second harlequin novel and vomits instead"

. . .

"I see tall office buildings and short wide palaces"

. . .

"pressing ridges into the roof of your mouth"

. . .

"foreign entities intermingling"

. . .

"I do not want to engage with the mise-en-scene"

. . .

"my arrival is ambiguous"

. . .

"is it okay to borrow something for later repurposing?"

. . .

"I lack the drive to do so"

. . .

"how many documents have you disregarded?"

. . .

"you are the witness of a vomiting"

. . .

"a seismologist says something about an oncoming hellscape"

. . .

"I cannot place myself within language"

. . .

"the severing of certain vestigial nerves"

. . .

"data amassing across a conductive surface"

. . .

"Tommyboy appearing and disappearing"

. . .

"I met a man who had managed to completely evade language"

. . .

"Tommyboy decides that he does not want to learn how to speak and that is okay"

. . .

"severing the connection between signifier and signified"

. . .

"living without a name"

. . .

"mangling the mechanical body of the car after its crash"

. . .

"the sun changes hues again"

. . .

"a doctor says that my eyes cannot detect cubism"

. . .

"encountering the object as itself"

. . .

"I do not know if it is in his nature or if this is new for him"

. . .

"I do not want to read Heidegger or Hegel or any of the prominent H's"

. . .

"everyone continues to mind their own business"

. . .

"places his lips over the face and tries to suck up the nutrients"

. . .

"it stretches when subjected to an increase in density"

"more has happened so time has moved with a greater speed"

. . .

"he is lost on me now"

. . .

"a doctor says that my eyes cannot detect treated panes of glass"

. . .

"time is affected by activity"

. . .

"do you remember Blondboy?"

. . .

"first off"

. . .

"it has been forever"

. . .

"but in reality no time at all"

. . .

"do you know one another?"

. . .

"a row of beheadings"

. . .

"let us begin again"

. . .

"mountain of raw meat and stone fruits"

. . .

(applause)

"rumors of a revisitation"

. . .

"it is difficult to distinguish between playful and serious"

. . .

"this is a known fact"

. . .

"the moment something is said"

. . .

"nobody has to know"

. . .

"the transition from space to land must be jarring"

. . .

"I no longer want to hear an answer"

. . .

"bus wading through asphalt"

. . .

"it is in the shape of a bull or ox"

"locomotion changes across mediums"

. . .

"a hundred headless woman"

. . .

"someone says something about a diorite altar"

. . .

"must everything be uttered from the same mouth?"

. . .

"in search of lost meaning"

. . .

(applause and laughter)

"it has become inaccessible without the proper equipment"

. . .

"there is too much now"

. . .

"a nightmare"

. . .

"I am forced to work in a different medium"

. . .

"a minotaure"

. . .

"motifs are resurrected from previous iterations of the text"

. . .

"the city is so loud right now"

. . .

"the American is a patronizing figure"

. . .

"smut-maker accepts this mockery and attempts to consume it"

. . .

"a policeman says that he is too old to hear the white noise"

. . .

"whether they accept this position or not"

. . .

"I want to be left with my own unresolved conclusions."

ACT 26

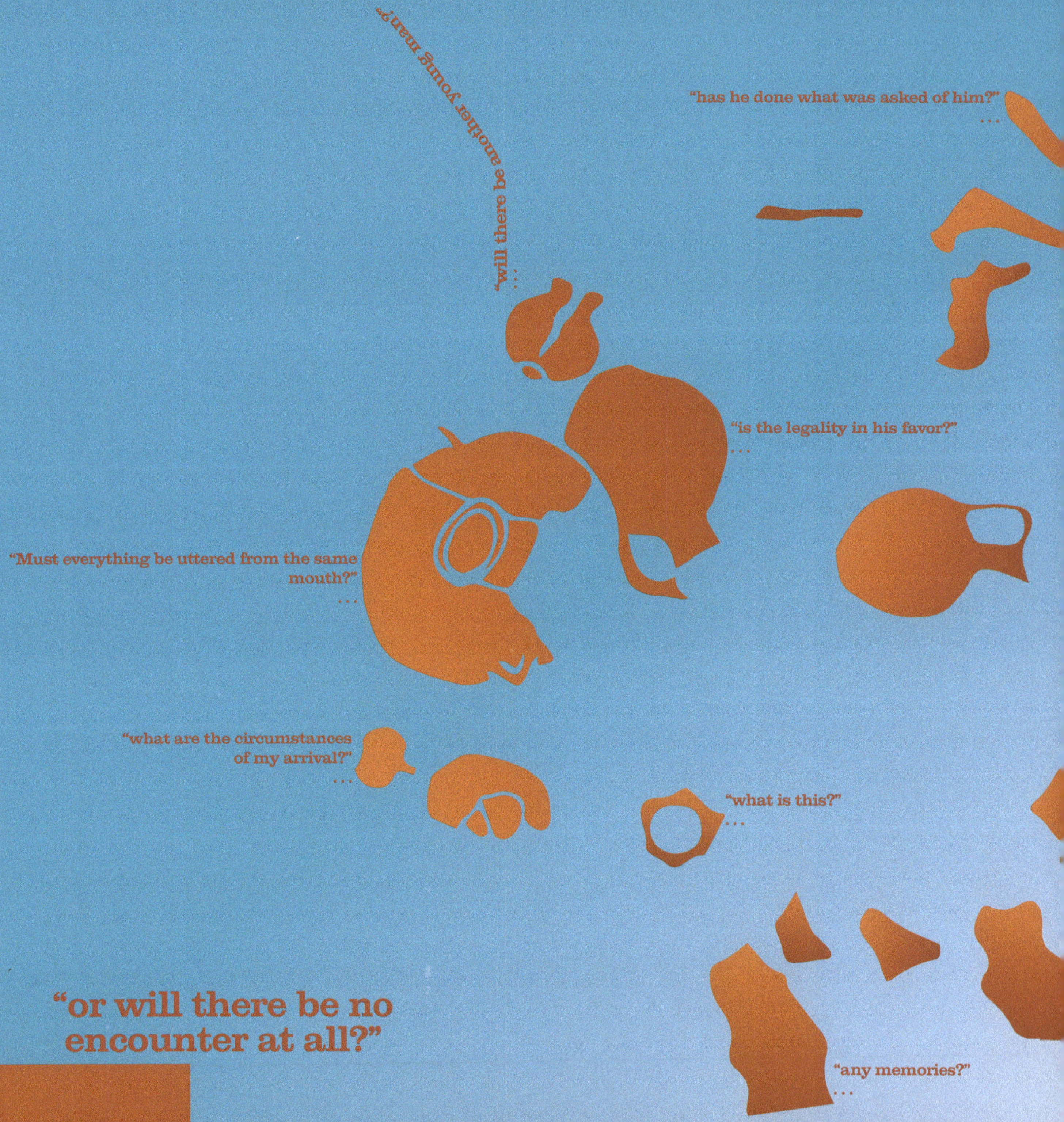

"or will there be no encounter at all?"

"what constitutes the connection between signifier and signified?"
. . .

"have you encountered the minotaure yet?"
. . .

"have you ever met someone so dense?"
. . .

"any dreams?"
. . .

"are you willing to sever your connection to something representative?"
. . .

"did the smut-maker do that?"
. . .

"is he familiar with these procedures?"
. . .

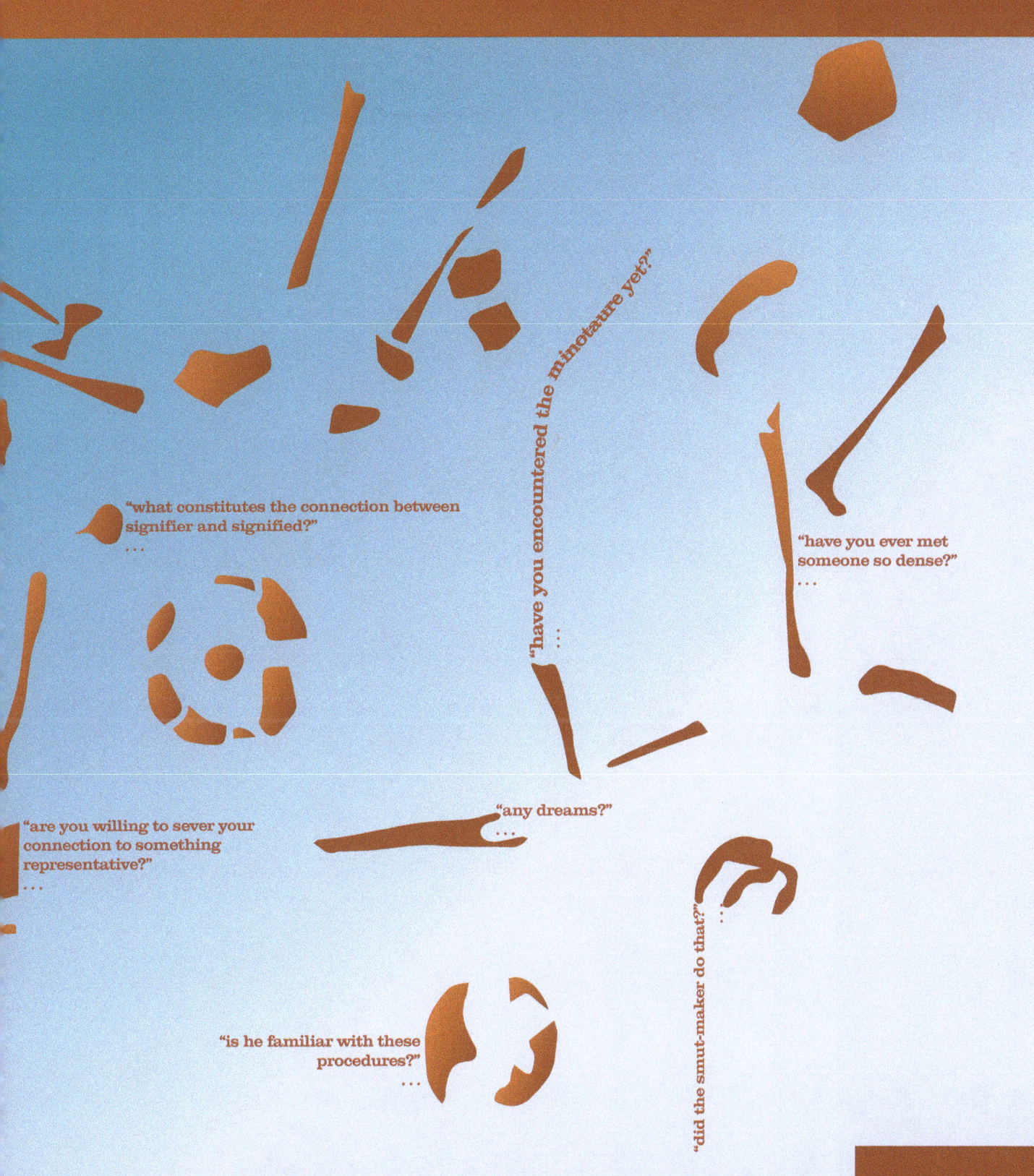

ACT 27

"I—you—yeah mean, uh, like is so know it, um, no okay."

. . . "Okay like, um, you... yeah no I... it so mean is uh know."

. . .

"You, uh, like mean no it is okay... so yeah, um, I know." . . .

"You? Yeah no... mean, um... okay I know, uh, is like so it."

. . .

"Uh okay, um, is I know no it you like so mean yeah."

. . .

"Like, so I mean you know okay, um, yeah, it is, no, uh."

. . .

"I like yeah you, is; know, uh, Like um mean okay it so no."

. . .

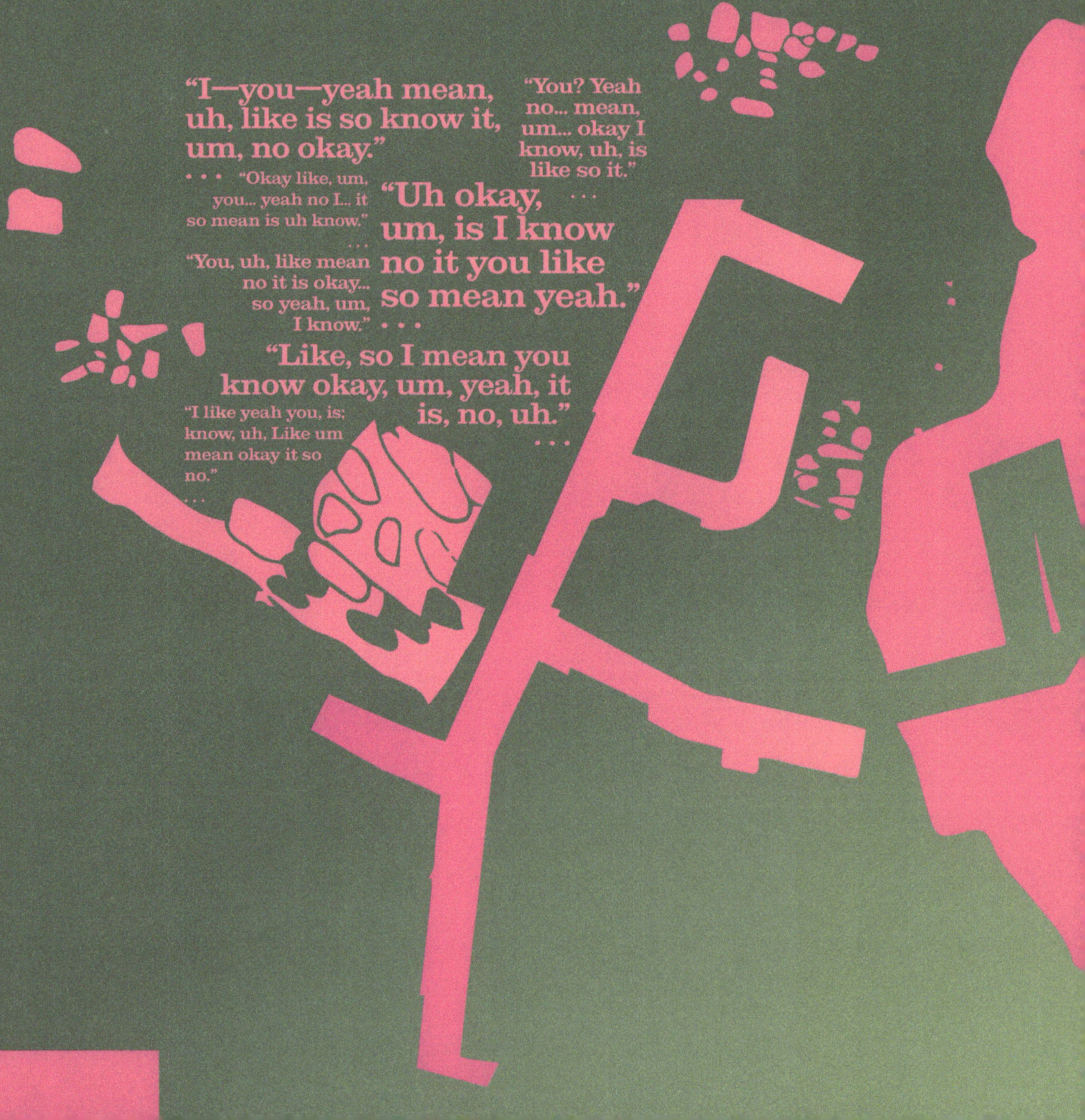

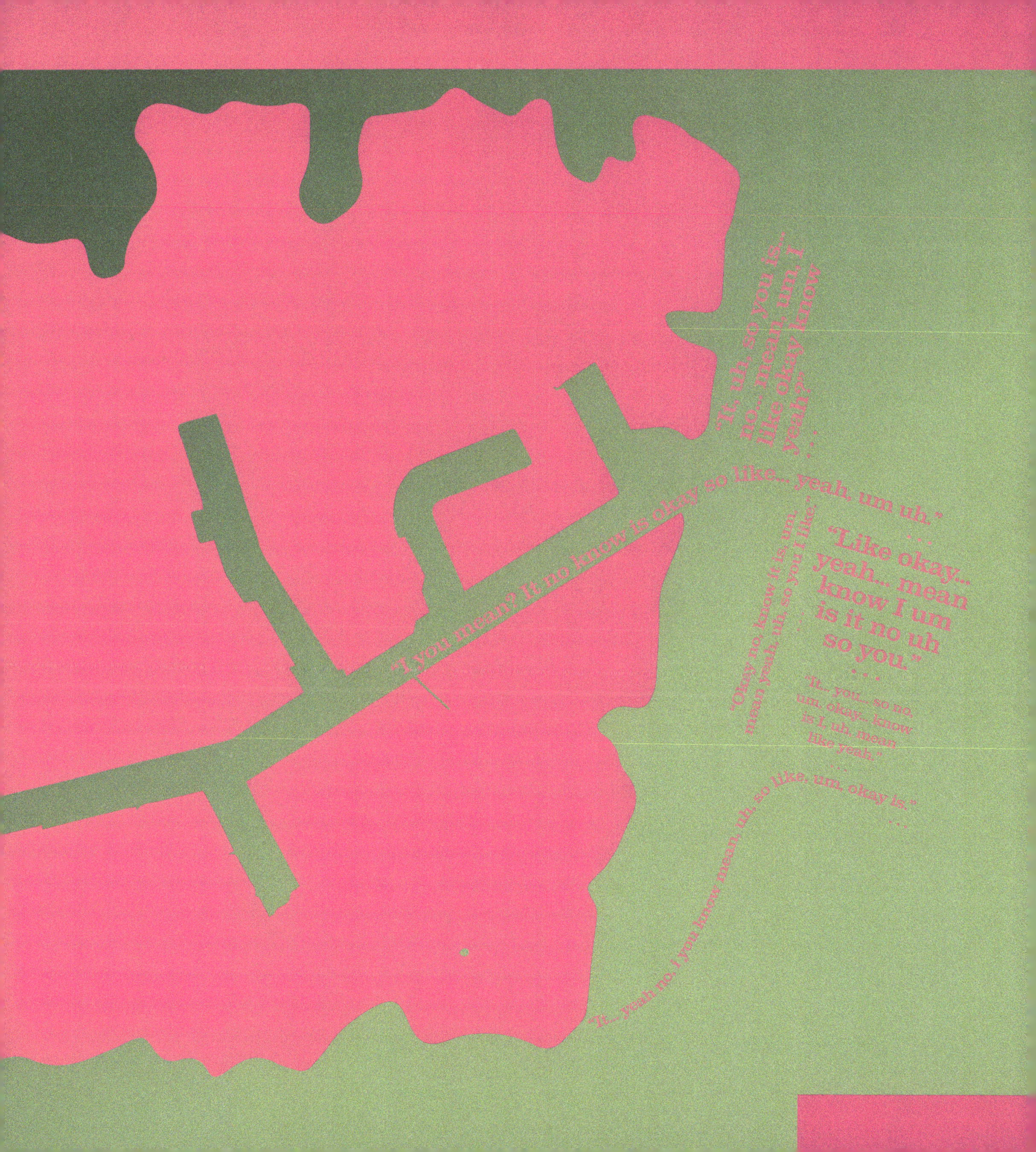
"It, uh, so you is... no... mean, um, I like okay know yeah?"
"I you mean? It no know is okay so like... yeah, um uh."
"Like okay... yeah... mean know I um is it no uh so you."
"Okay no, know it is, um, mean yeah, uh, so you I like."
"It... you... so no, um, okay... know is I, uh, mean like yeah."
"It... yeah no, I you know mean, uh, so like, um, okay is."

ACT 28

"I feel possessed" . . .

"gas welling underneath the surface"

. . .

"Tommyboy and smut-maker fuck on the floor" . . .

"pressing against the underside of the meniscus"

. . .

"debris pulled into air from the vacuum"

. . .

"Xenobiologist tests for unknown sediment in the water"

. . .

"I suffer from symptoms of pareidolia"

. . .

"every symbol reveals itself at once"

. . .

"the remnan dissolvin brine

. . .

"before I could say anything at all"

. . .

"plumes of fabric"

. . .

"ilium arcing its angle"

. . .

"they tangle in a cradle of limbs"

. . .

"a field of anuses"

. . .

"hips bruised and fragile"

. . .

"violent and jarring"

. . .

"every action blunt and vulgar"

. . .

"someone steps away for a cigarette"

. . .

"it is rendered int haptic world"

. . .

"a thought is broken down into its immobile segments"

. . .

"as a child he is not taught to count with roman numerals"

. . .

"not Blondboy

. .

"a system of schools"

. . .

"a carpenter constructs uncanny habitats for her offspring"

. . .

"blood and flesh endless in its departure from the skull"

. . .

"city drowning in the ma of its construction"

. . .

"I see the coming of a great red flood"

. . .

"not smut-maker"

. . .

"the subject on their cha anatom

. . .

"Tommyboy says that no one knows how to make him cum"

. . .

"not the Mex avant-gardis he married"

. . .

"pink matter spills from their head"

. . .

"entrails sloping onto the floor"

. . .

"there is too much now"

. . .

"the skull opened and revealed to the air"

. . .

"contaminants seep into the water"

. . .

"has it formed grooves along your tongue and throat?"

. . .

"have you read the Wittgenstein?"

. . .

"he sits on the edge of the bed"

. . .

n

other
urbates
nst the
board"

. . .

"with a certain irreducible length and width"

. . .

e

he thought-image"

. . .

"brow bone a split tectonic plate"

. . .

"not you"

. . .

es
g

"no dreams no memories"

. . .

"dead birds rise to the top of a well"

. . .

"whom he has avoided since the ceremony"

. . .

"there is a difference between pipes and wells"

. . .

"narrator-fool Mike Corrao coughs into a garbage can"

. . .

"pipes begin to crack and decay"

. . .

"between movement and stasis."

"Tommyboy sings something beautiful"

. . .

ACT 29

"conspiratorial in its posture"

. . .

"narrator-fool enters Tommyboy"

"their dynamic
feels out of
order"

. . .

"but it is
not"

. . .

"if it is short I will write it on one short roll of paper"

. . .

"my hands carry
an unfamiliar
scent"

. . .

"00000"

. . .

"have you seen
the rockets
firing off?"

. . .

"do you
think
smut-
maker will
leave?"

. . .

"it becomes
a long
novel"

. . .

"lift your skinny hands
to heaven"

. . .

"someone has been
activating missile
silos in the middle
of the night"

. . .

"Tommyboy tells a joke about taints and cowboys"

. . .

"old cop writes a note about
diorite altars"

. . .

"we
do not
know
each
other"

. . .

"you are not a product of the
schizopastoral as you have so desperately
tried to convince me"

. . .

"a garden of teeth"

. . .

"it comes with a
certain vernacular"

. . .

"antennae
protruding from
intercostals"

. . .

"this is a
disease of
the mind"

. . .

"silhouette standing
at the precipice of the
obelisk"

. . .

"he curls himself into the fetal
position"

. . .

"00000"

. . .

this is not a real concern"

. . .

"if a work of fiction is long I will write it on one long roll of paper"

. . .

"he does not answer"

. . .

"the minotaure permeates your memory"

"and you think that it might be a sign"

. . .

"crowds disperse"

. . .

"high schoolers loiter outside of a gas station"

. . .

"a row of succulents"

. . .

"you are concerned that this creature has been placed inside of you"

. . .

"the city is reduced to its architecture"

. . .

"breathes in monotone"

. . .

"someone asks him when he is going to go home"

"a horse collapses in the center of the road"

. . .

"you ask yourself what it must look like"

. . .

"Tommyboy says that he does not like this arrangement"

. . .

"you reconsider this image of the schizopastoral"

. . .

"it is only speculation"

. . .

"and each answer you arrive at feels unsatisfactory"

. . .

"it is moving in reverse."

. . .

"the Mexican avant-gardist does not call the apartment"

"he waits until Tommyboy is ready"

. . .

ACT 30

"the third time?"
. . .
"constructs a cosmic apparatus"
"I remain passive." . . .

“There must have been six or seven of them”
• • •
“what is it now?”
• • •
“wo await the arrival of a cult”
• • •
“the resurrection of various messianic characters”
• • •
“Tommyboy treats the bruises that have welled on his forehead”
• • •
“Sun Ra arcs across the solarscape”
• • •
“we do not carry out any irreversible actions”
• • •
“it is a day of rest”
• • •
“my hands have become prone to bleeding lately”
• • •
“the third iteration?”
• • •
“he blames a delayed reaction to the initial collision”
• • •

ACT 31

"any memories?"

. . .

“Any dreams?”

. . .

“something
pooling
underneath
the
surface.”

ACT 32

"you
ask another
question about the
schizopastoral but at
this point it feels more
like an excuse than a
reality"
. . .

"Blondboy"
. . .
"difference and differ
. . .

"wading
through
a sea o
corpse
. . .

"smut-maker
critiques the
connection between
this term and his
second harlequin
novel"
. . .

"weight growing"
. . .
"each co

"pink matter
flourishing in
haptic landscape"
. . .
"the critique is empty of
meaning"
. . .
"I am caught in the act of
decomposing"
. . .

"forgive me for this"
. . .
"to be born"
. . .

"regardless"
. . .
"the key to learning
is
sensory
feedback"

"Dante drags
his tongue over
volcanic soil"

. . . "mentions of CCTV" . . .
. . .

"suspicious
underground
activities"

. . . "launch codes
are rendered by a larger
neural network"

"an untrustworthy
hegemonic
machine"

. . .

"she remembers a tower of corpses"

. . .

"a woman stood outside of
the initial impact"

. . .

"Tommyboy lays
on top of smut-
maker"

. . .

"that there will be
an inevitable
third boy"

. . .

"someone
says that
they
desire to
remain
out
of reach"

. . .

"or its new
American
equivalent"

. . .

"the
minotaure"

. . .

"Dante lingers
unread
in the
periphery"

. . .

"paradiso
slouching
towards
Bethlehem"

. . .

"he looks
down at
himself"

. . .

"and
considers
the
penis."

"there is news
of movement"

. . .

"footage courtesy
of governmental
security
cameras"

. . .

ation a new missile firing off at dusk"

. . .

"fears that this will pass" . . .

"perched as bird or gargoyle"

meone says
at they saw
ommyboy
lingering near
the laundromat"

. . .

"removing
evidence of
impact"

. . .

"whoever else"

. . .

"suspicious
agents
treading
through blast
zones"

. . .

"slope
between hills
of ass"

. . .

"the
nude
umbra"

. . .

"the implications of
their arrival
and departure"

. . .

"there is no reason to pay
attention"

. . .

"Tommyboy
remains at the
front of my
mind"

. . .

ACT 33

"I begin my deterioration"

. . .

"and be replaced by artificial facsimiles"

. . .

"limb to text"

. . .

"bathroom"

. . .

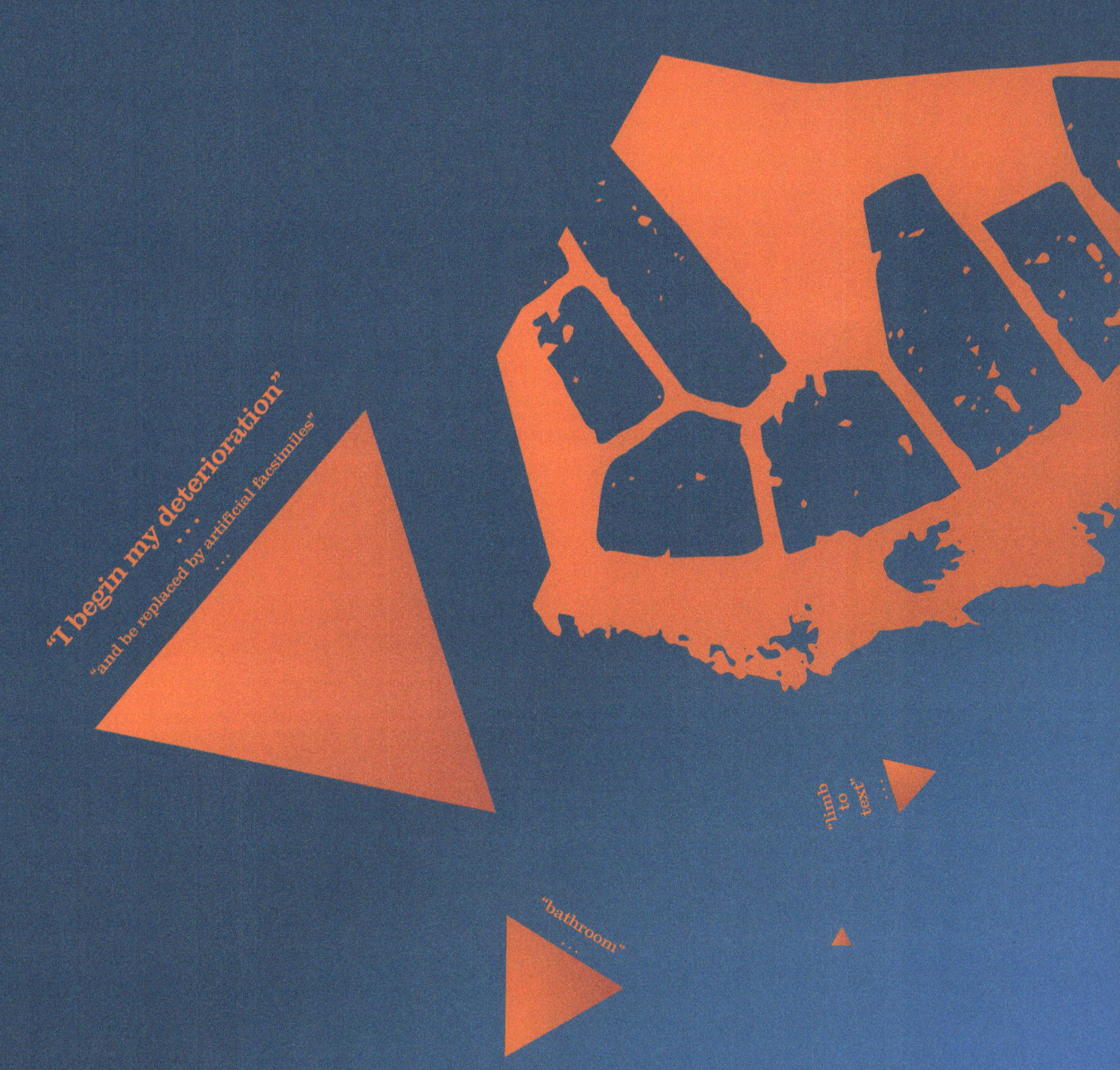

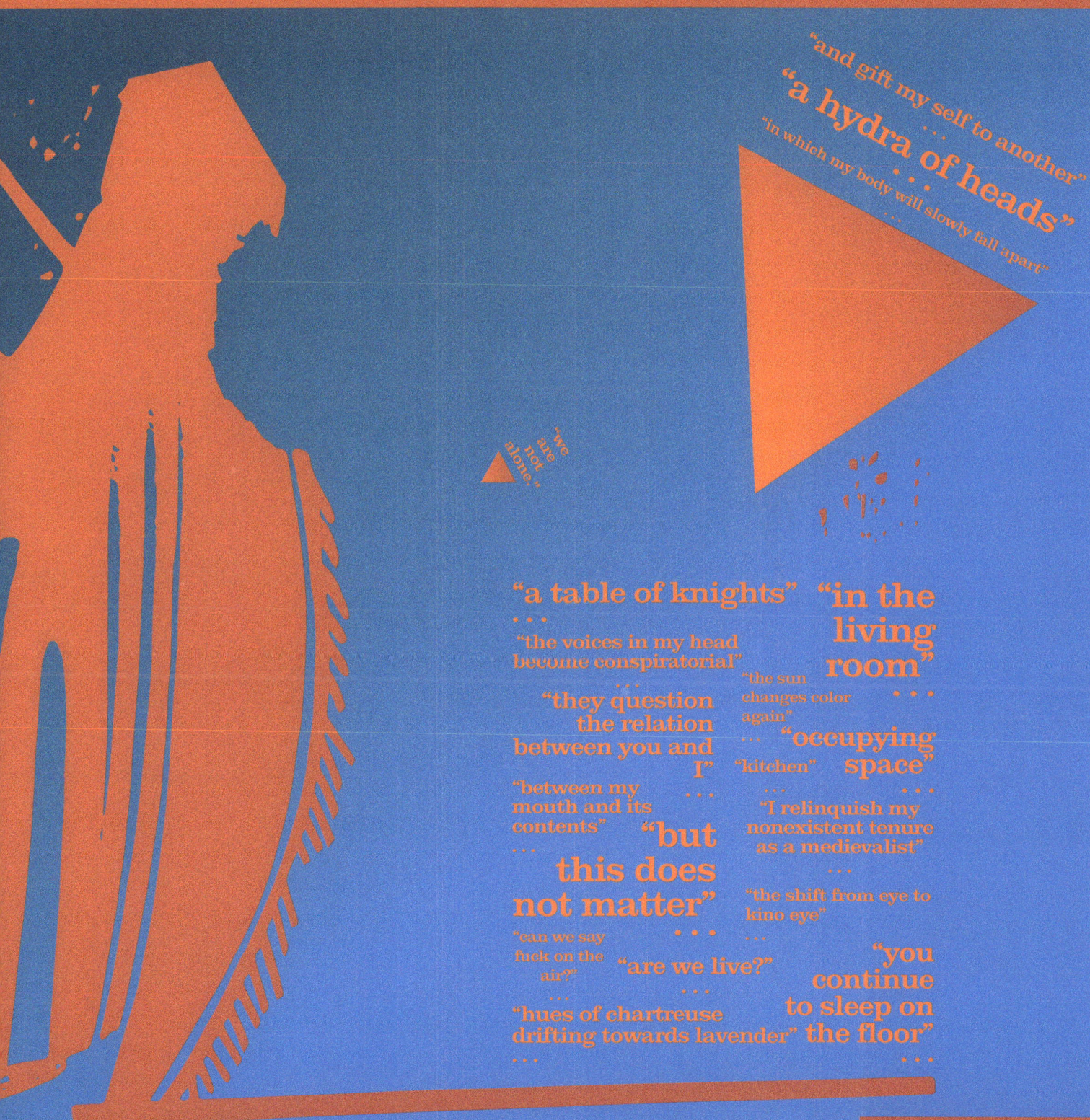

"and gift my self to another"

. . .

"a hydra of heads"

. . .

"in which my body will slowly fall apart"

. . .

"we are not alone."

"a table of knights"

. . .

"the voices in my head become conspiratorial"

. . .

"they question the relation between you and I"

. . .

"between my mouth and its contents"

. . .

"but this does not matter"

. . .

"can we say fuck on the air?"

. . .

"are we live?"

. . .

"hues of chartreuse drifting towards lavender"

. . .

"in the living room"

. . .

"the sun changes color again"

. . .

"occupying space"

. . .

"kitchen"

. . .

"I relinquish my nonexistent tenure as a medievalist"

. . .

"the shift from eye to kino eye"

. . .

"you continue to sleep on the floor"

. . .

ACT 34

"There is no debt to be paid" "Tommyboy" "when are you going to leave him behind?" "a chain of apes" "98235?"
. . . "your decisions are your own" . . . "Blondboy" . . . "you begin to feel concerned"
. . . "no one is ever around for too long" . . . "the sun changing hues" . . . "a series of empty mistakes" . . .
"you're gonna carry that weight" . . . "each new iteration of desire" . . . "do you feel the desire to eat him out?" . . . "a pack of wolves" . . . "moved by an arcane gesture" . . . "this was a collision" . . .
"can you remember the names?" . . . "I do not learn from my mistakes" . . .
"manifesting in the pink matter" . . . "Deadboy" . . . "it might be time to leave" . . . "Tommyboy says that he is not ready to leave" . . .
"all of the tenements woke at once" . . . "smoking a cigarette and sliding their bodies back in through the entryway" . . . "wallet remaining in my pocket" . . . "government websites are redressed in futurist imagery" . . .
"every doorway an altar to the yonic" . . . "my name is stolen" . . . "it is scratched off of my ID and placed elsewhere" . . . "you ask when he will be" . . .
"sounds of the mechanisms inside your walls" . . . "00000" . . . "but this does not fully materialize" . . . "there is too much here" . . . "silh of a airp. . . .
"synthetic growths clinging to the inner drywall" . . . "we are the same" . . . "the apartment begins to smell like candle wax" . . .
"tin drum echoing from space" . . . "in search of lost meaning" . . . "there is too much here now" . . . "motifs aligned as photographs on corkboard" . . . "00000" . . .
"Tommyboy rides a rocket over the horizon" . . .
"deshelling pistachios over the sink" . . . "in the removal of these vestigial limbs you seek a more synthetic alternative" . . . "a policeman writing notes about divine death on his notepad" . . . "where the roc . . .
"an attempt to depict the image of god" . . . "humans are quick to die" . . . "there was no accident involved" . . .
"static or a series of blotches" . . . "flesh is poor building materials" . . . "what kind of message do you want to send him?" . . . "no one does a good job" . . .
"a face with no particular importance" . . . "avant-gardists outside of densely packed cafes" . . . "I cannot remember our beginning" . . .
"you do not believe in its existence" . . . "and I do not blame you" . . . "every object and subject in its likeness" . . . "it is or of s

te
ding

8679?"
. . .

(pause)

ead for?"

"I fall
ep on
ouch"
. . .

ot know
he rockets
going"
. . .

matter
lation"
. . .

"le
petite
mort"
. . .

"shrine to a
genderless car
crash"
. . .

"producing
new smut in
reality
and mimesis"
. . .

"it is
difficult
to say"
. . .

"how many collages have come
together here?"
. . .

"Tommyboy is married
to an avant-gardist from
Mexico and it is not my
place to change things"
. . .

"Sun
Ra
curving
along
the sky"
. . .

"matching
the angle of the
surface below
him"
. . .

"every voice
lifts at once"
. . .

"I do not have
the right or the
power to do so"
. . .

"people
do not
fuck
strangers
unless
they
have the
reason
to"
. . .

"smut-maker is only
concerned with sex
and harlequin
novels"
. . .

"where
did Tommyboy come
from?"
. . .

"even if that reason is
pleasure or curiosity."

ACT 35

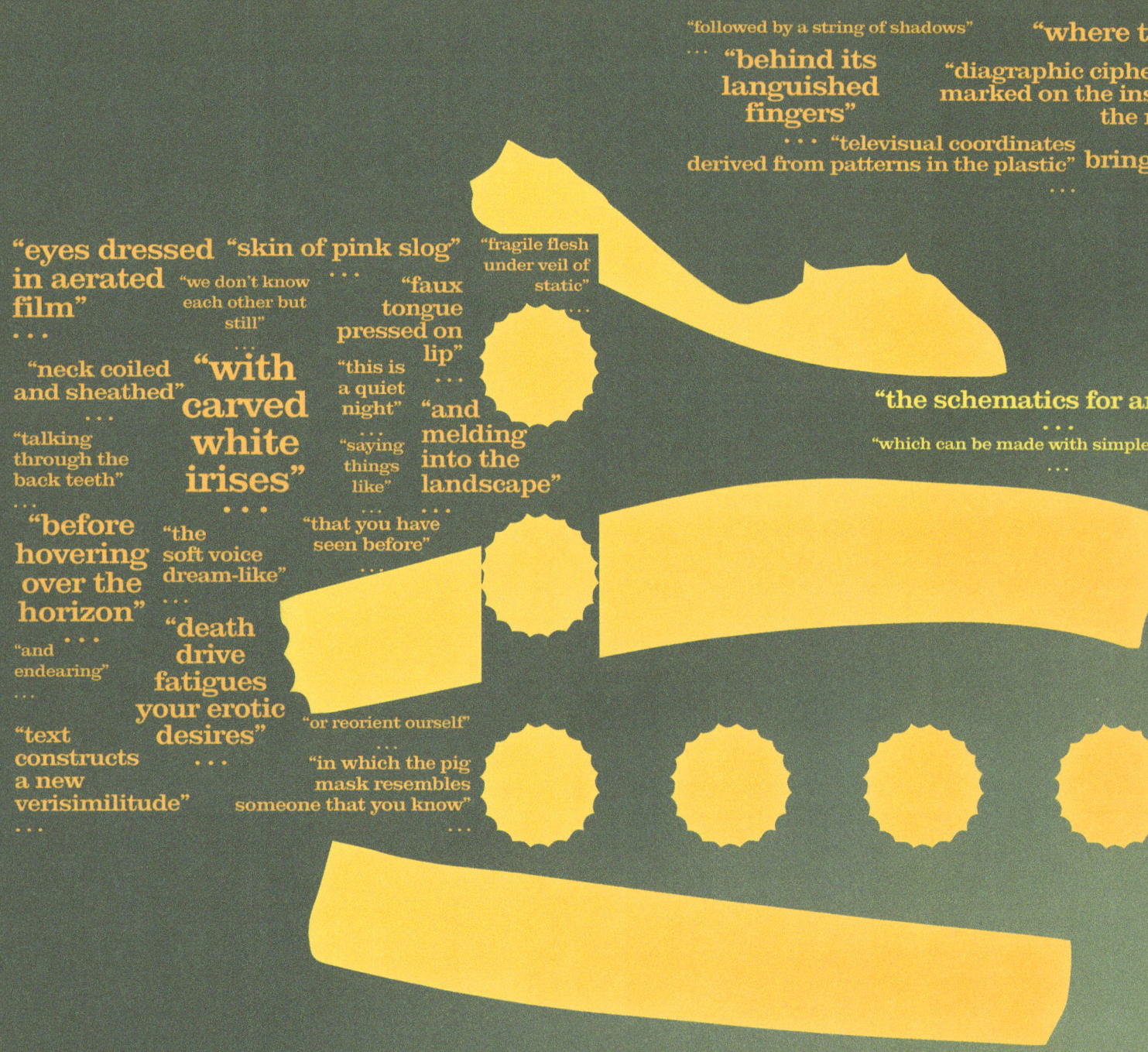

"followed by a string of shadows"

. . . "behind its languished fingers"

. . . "televisual coordinates derived from patterns in the plastic"

. . .

"where th

"diagraphic ciphe
marked on the ins
the r

bring

"eyes dressed in aerated film"

. . .

"neck coiled and sheathed"

. . .

"talking through the back teeth"

. . .

"before hovering over the horizon"

. . .

"and endearing"

. . .

"text constructs a new verisimilitude"

. . .

"skin of pink slog"

"we don't know each other but still"

. . .

"with carved white irises"

. . .

"the soft voice dream-like"

. . .

"death drive fatigues your erotic desires"

. . .

. . .

"faux tongue pressed on lip"

. . .

"this is a quiet night"

. . .

"saying things like"

. . .

"and melding into the landscape"

. . .

"that you have seen before"

. . .

"fragile flesh under veil of static"

. . .

"or reorient ourself"

. . .

"in which the pig mask resembles someone that you know"

. . .

"the schematics for ar

. . .

"which can be made with simple

. . .

annot be seen by anyone”

. . .

“two investigators your attention”

. . .

r”

ls”

“they do not act like real investigators”

. . .

“voice obfuscated by a growing white noise”

. . .

“false projections radiate from the beheaded animal”

. . .

“where to locate them”

. . .

“and used for purposes that are not necessarily important to you”

. . .

“but it doesn’t mean anything”

. . .

“they do not act like real investigators”

. . .

“you tell them that you haven’t seen the mask before”

. . .

“still alive and breathing”

. . .

“what they contain”

. . .

“the pig mask infiltrates your dreams”

. . .

“and begins reorganizing the data in your skull”

. . .

“but it is difficult to move”

. . .

“the place where you and i stand has become frail”

. . .

“they leave it with you”

. . .

“your new skull-data reveals to you”

. . .

“Stranger slumped in pig mask”

. . .

“and floral nightgown”

. . .

“hands fluttering under linen”

. . .

“orchids weaving”

. . .

“they say something about psychogeographic techniques”

. . .

“swaying gracefully towards”

. . .

“the place where you and I stand”

. . .

“but that you feel the desire to be the cause of.”

. . .

“posture curved forward”

. . .

ACT 36

"Time moves episodically"

. . .

"montage of necessary information"

. . .

"he wanders between laundromat and cafe"

. . .

"the duration of something cinematic"

. . .

"a group of ambitious architects assembles a tower of polymer compartments"

. . .

"shifting between past present and future"

. . .

"Tommyboy crashes down to earth and no longer knows who he is"

. . .

"sleeps on my bed or couch"

. . .

"my vision is static"

. . .

"speaks the prophetic offhandedly"

. . .

"I learn to fear the blackness behind this screen"

. . .

"someone says they are moving into a home made from uncanny geometries"

. . .

"becomes fascinated by the resilience of a polymer structure."

"someone says that the minotaure will not be arriving"
. . .

"what did the eye doctor tell you?"
. . .

"they are labeled as a consultant in the accompanying NDA"
. . .

"the schizopastoral is edited and redefined as a landscape of complexification"
. . .

"Applause and laughter
. . .

"turning the tundra into something volcanic"
. . .

"I have just received a message"
. . .

"Tommyboy distinguishes between what he loves and what he is attracted to"
. . .

"shift from legs to numb"
. . .

"I cannot stop the riverrun"
. . .

"not soon anyways"
. . .

"narrator-fool the product of some archaic seduction"
. . .

"how thoroughly do you believe that you are being documented?"
. . .

"a large novel is described as Joycean by an affiliated professor"
. . .

"it is not a sequel"
. . .

"your head is deterritorialized and placed on another plateau"
. . .

"that your movements are being recorded and archived"
. . .

"smut-maker begrudgingly begins his third harlequin novel"
. . .

"an editor is brought on to verify or dismiss this statement"
. . .

"that they will be analyzed and used against you"
. . .

"by means of radio wave and interception"
. . .

"in the tradition of Deleuze and Guattari"
. . .

"flood of pitch slowly absorbing into the soil"
. . .

"an apartment constructed from fake wood"
. . .

"someone on the television says that it has almost been two decades since Y2K"
. . .

"savant mummified in linens"
. . .

"work begins at the mise-en-scene"
. . .

"a meteorite ascending into the vacuum"
. . .

"drapes over scaffolding of bone"
. . .

"what comes from space will eventually return"
. . .

"how can you not?"
. . .

"your conception of the schizopastoral is criticized for its underdevelopment"
. . .

"this fear of digitalization of our existence"
. . .

"the he that permeates space and time"
. . .

"tower of televisions"
. . .

"everything goes pitch black"
. . .

"I believe him when he says that he came from space"
. . .

"my father was staffed as an emergency electrical responder"
. . .

"paranoid speech filtered through video installation"
. . .

"mass of flesh"
. . .

"in an era of computational primitivism"
. . .

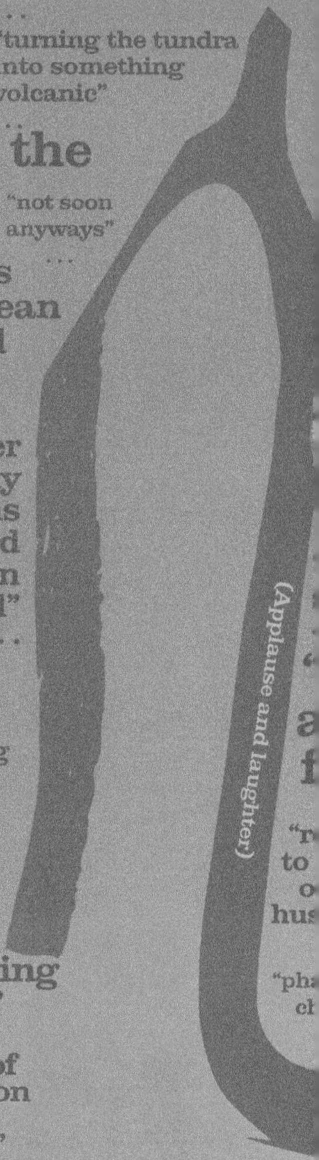

am unable to see what is in front of me the whole time"

"heels digging into mattress"

"because it is beneficial to remain invisible"

"this does not mean anything to you"

y that ive e my can mp

"every movement a bodily response"

"smut-maker flexing his stomach and jaw"

"I've heard that somewhere before"

"he will leave"

"they sit across from one another and talk about previous encounters"

"machinery chirps like birds"

"it is inevitable"

minotaure

"smut-maker attempts to reorganize his theoretical framework"

"is tracked across page count"

"comparing the former to the latter"

"Xiu Xiu weaving basket"

"in search of lost meanings"

"vomiting blackblood onto trade paperbacks."

"I remain sitting"

"Tommyboy drags his tongue across neck"

"Tommyboy says that he is going to leave"

r l s e" ect "

"horizon rolling into a flat line"

"anchoring body to foundation"

"Bolaño mutters as he shuffles into a side alley"

"says that you should shave your face"

"an autopsy is performed to better understand the mirroring alien anatomy"

"in the tradition of Bergson"

"he was twenty-seven"

"but I am always certain it is there when I see it"

"people've got to be suspicious"

"it's lost on me now"

"you either turn twenty-seven or you die"

"I do not know how this label is acquired"

"yelps and tries again"

"and crawls onto me"

l a "

"bodies draped across fray wooden furniture"

"fat accumulating at bend"

"Herzog moaning solar flares"

"circumnavigated by means of duration"

"Tommyboy assumes the position of the he"

"it is natural to feel an aversion to such activities"

"a poet mentions her fascination with guns and birds"

"gatekeeper of a linear time"

"his face a façade of static"

"as I will be"

"Tommyboy enters narrator-fool"

"tension holding mass to surface"

"better at being than I"

"I do not know whether or not I am being dishonest"

"I do not"

"there is something too revealing about the *longue duree* of your waiting around"

"I should not"

"says that he will continue to work within these constraints"

"I believe him when he says that he is from outer space"

"no one turns on the television"

"poetically tissue dwells"

"it is unsettling and intimate"

"saying that a bullet flies in the same arc as a canary"

"when he tells me that he does not want to sleep on the couch"

"memory of Blondboy standing outside of the laundromat"

"sitting on the toilet for hours"

"you stare at a mobile device"

"I am told by an unfamiliar avant-gardist"

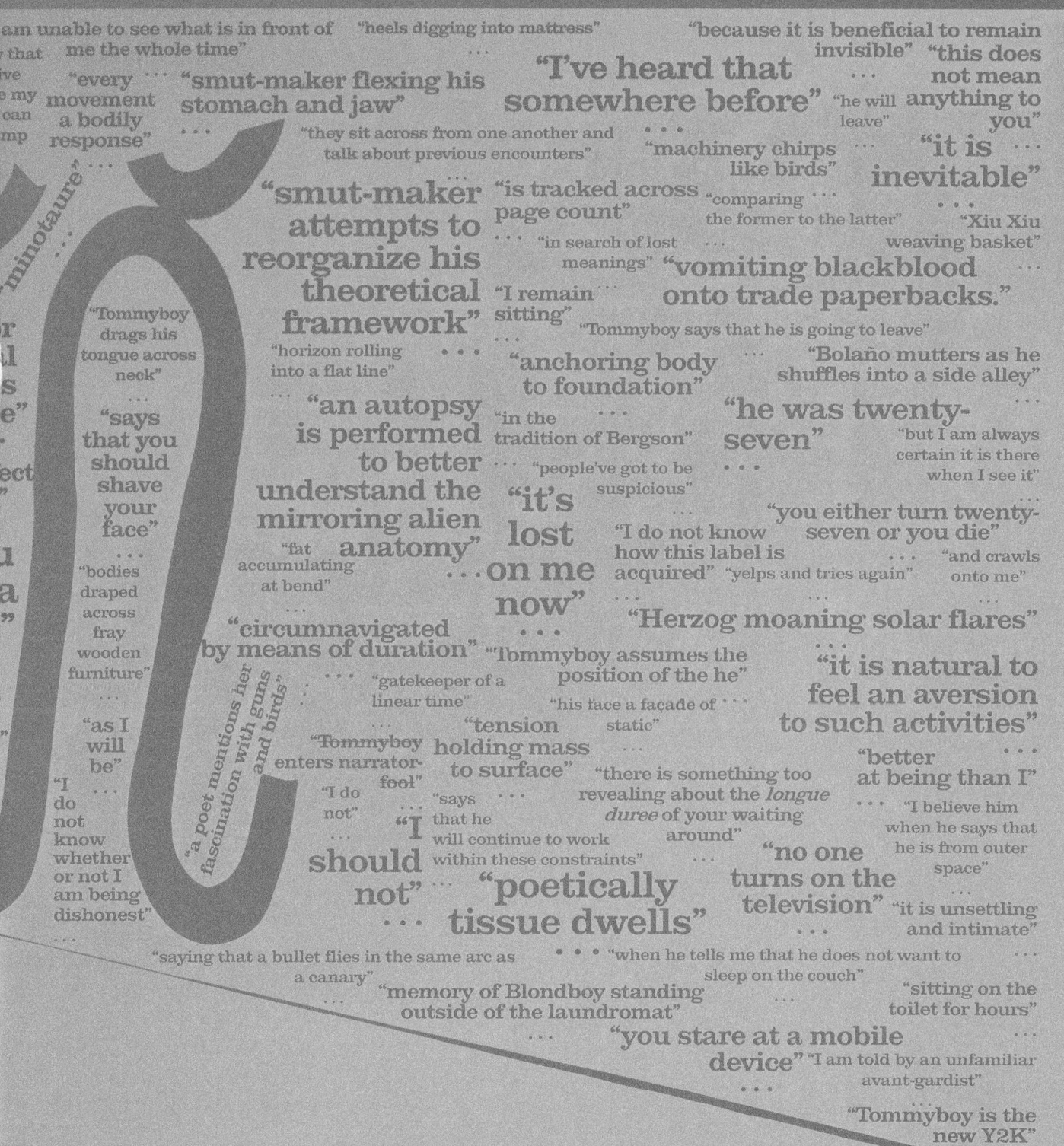

"Tommyboy is the new Y2K"

ACT 38

"Mike Corrao watches rockets fire off in the middle of the night"

. . . "any dreams?" . . .

"any memories?"

. . . "the sun changes from orange to yellow to redpink"

. . .

"wisps of light flowing behind as sentient tendrils"

. . .

"a government official says that there is nothing strange happening"

. . .

"his face is projected onto an unpaid actor"

. . .

"someone with similar bone structure and mannerisms"

. . .

"three days pass"

. . .

"the policeman writes a note about rockets on his notepad"

. . .

"an impromptu topography of the city"

. . .

"are you becoming tired?"

. . .

"can you keep up?"

. . .

"language organized into triangles"

. . .

"onto another medium"

. . .

"boulder laid across the width of his shoulders"

. . . "you're gonna carry that weight"

. . .

"of its simulation"

. . .

"there are too many meanings now"

. . .

"how many collages have been created now?"

. . .

"too many ways to interpret this act"

. . .

"difference and difference."

"three or four sheets of graphing paper"

. . .

"everything coded with an undetectable cipher"

. . .

ACT 39

"flirts with the remaining avant-gardists"

. . . "but loses interest in th

role"

"every fragment coalesces center of the stage"

. . .

"Tommyboy sitting across from screen"

. . .

"digital static" "00000"

. . .

"lag time and malfunctioning playheads"

. . .

. . . "he returns to space"

"abrupt and without warning"

. . .

. . .

"he attempts to predict the future but is wrong when the answer arrives"

. . .

"a matrix of fibres"

. . .

"she is related to

"just at their heads"

. . .

"time has already begun to pass"

. . .

"an old cop slowly typing on his terminal"

. . .

"duration permeates my sense of place"

. . .

"evidence locker bloated and unstable"

"smut-maker performs his personality"

. . .

"do you remember the car crash we saw a few months ago?"

. . .

"and the metallic bodies tangled together"

. . .

. . . "a rumor begins that Tommyboy catalyzed the rocket season"

. . .

"when two sedans collided into one another"

. . .

"hairs tangled between their heads"

. . .

ntarily pretends that he is an investiga-tor or a detective"
. . .

"a manifesto is written"
. . .

"is later discarded"
. . .

"a low frequency drones"
. . .

"carrying weight over telephone wires"
. . .

"my dictation continues."
. . .

"we enter the era of post-Tommyboy"
. . .

"00000"
. . .

"jaw pulled towards the ground"
. . .

"the rising hum"
. . .

"hangs outside of a cafe"
. . .

"discarding of language"
. . .

"mouth swelling with weight of vocal chords"
. . .

"I desire a return to object"
. . .

"the reclamation of my substance"
. . .

air of architects living outside of Paris"
. . .

"without thinking about anything"
. . .

"00000"
. . .

"every launch across the last month"
. . .

"that have slowed down since his departure"
. . .

"that began with his arrival"
. . .

"a woman at the state building refuses to acknowledge this"
. . .

"she says that it is above her pay grade"
. . .

"he vomits into the toilet at work"
. . .

"after departure"
. . .

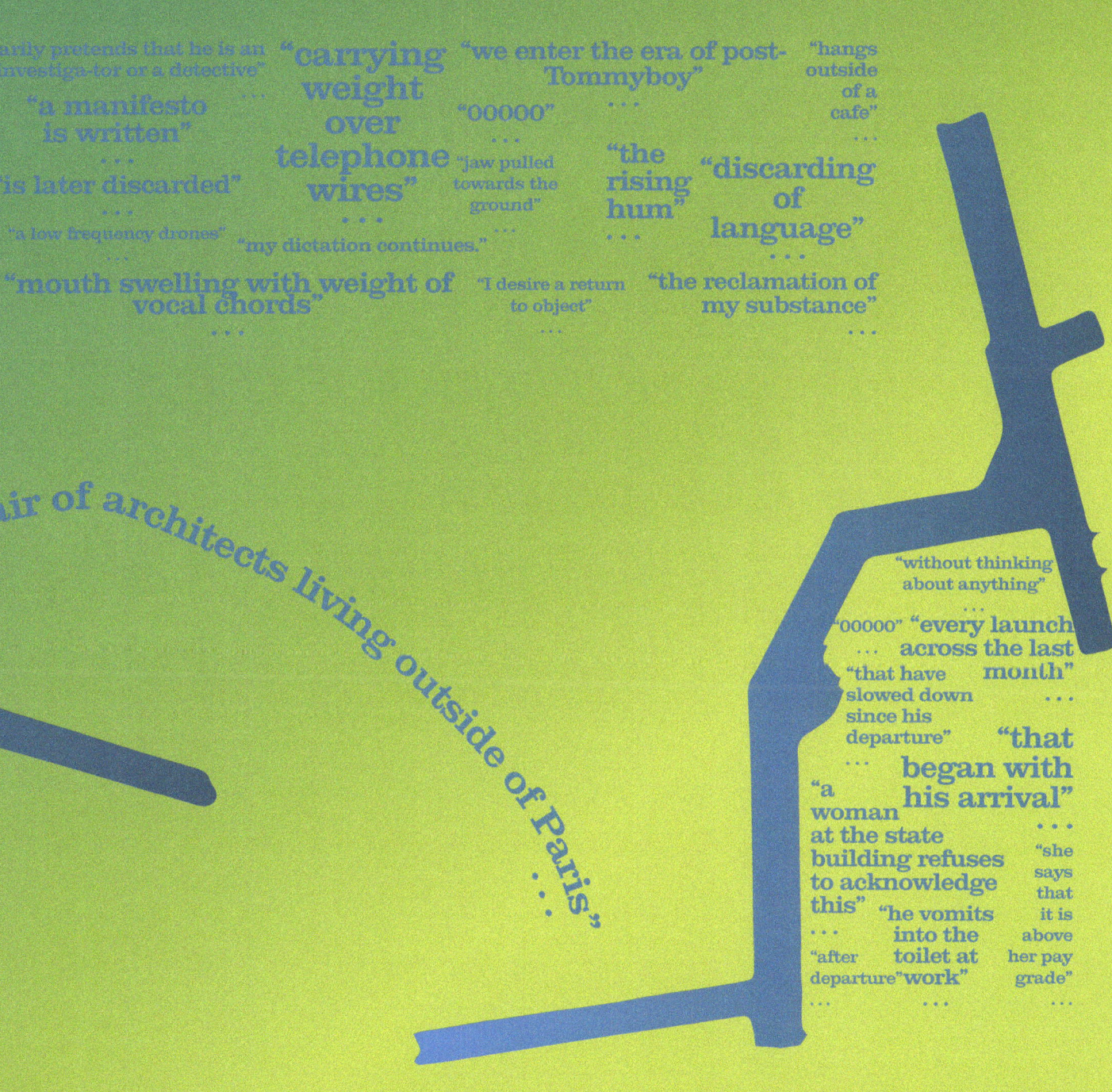

ACT 40

"I display myself as space"

"everybody weeps"

. . .

"I am scared of nothin

"two academics write an essay mapping the shift from haptic to digital"

"and you"

. . .

"the pl you sta

. . .

. . .

. . .

"projecting forms"

. . .

"I am scared of being" . . .

"carrying nomadic essence through each new portal"

. . .

"cinema is of its capit

. . .

. . .

"welcome to the digital badlands"

"witness to the becoming-bear"

. . .

"but its influence will p nonetheless"

. . .

"it is not where you have been projected to"

"heavy set mammal dragged through the Midwest"

. . .

. . .

"tufts of fur"

. . .

. . .

"hair tangled in the residue of disembodied voices"

"selling cursed artifacts"

. . .

"luxury editio file-bound facsi

. . .

"the spectral pla slowly renders"

. . .

"the rising sound of brass instrumentation"

. . .

"someone mentions the schizopastoral and he says that he has yet to clearly identify it"

"this is not importa

. . .

. . .

. . . "saxophone and trumpet and french horn singing"

"a forest is constructed around narrator-fool"

. . .

"an expedition"

. . .

"my patron saint singing"

. . .

"the desk where he has written his first three harlequin novels"

. . .

. . .

"he hears jazz playing in the distance"

"caravan drums and optimistic brass"

"but it is r

. . .

"echo of pooling w

. . .

. . .

"wandering astrally"

"rising jazz" . . .

. . .

. . .

"a spectral form projected onto a different plane"

"trees are tall and fibrous"

. . .

"their physica becoming inva

. . .

"the clock murmurs in

. . .

"an old movie theater closes its doors"

. . .

"bass thudding like woodcutter's axe"

"two c filling

. . .

. . . . . .

"a prayer is made at the base of an extravagant relief"

"the forming of a chain of metaphors"

ss"
where

"a car crashes into the lake"

. . .

"you cannot create water without creating the water crash"

"there is a subsequent overstimulation"

"is he somewhere else now?"

"metonyms fractalizing themselves"

"you've annotated a book before reading it"

ripped
e"

"violent and jarring"

"his mouth remains ajar."

"in search of lost meanings"

"where is Tommyboy?"

"this does not feel right"

ate

"jagged in shape"

"someone thudding and mouthing"

"an overproduction of meaning"

"the world is abstract and expressionist"

ound smut-maker"

"I cannot have dreams"

"the yet-to-be read Wittgenstein"

of
es"

"details materialize"

"distant jazz"

"Sun Ra croons about the intergalactic"

"a row of chairs"

"bleach dripping from tip of leaf"

"memories resurfacing"

"smut-maker moaning in anger"

"he projects himself into the somewhere else"

"I think that this could be the end"

"yet here we are"

and
flecks of dust"

"a lack of
unctuation"

"water tearing paint from metal"

. . . an altar is built in memory of the late Paul Virilio . . .

"

"projecting from apartment to unrealized forests"

sit at their desks
paperwork"

ACT 41

"opaque and speckled"
. . .
"kino eye gazes down upon my apartment"
. . .
"black and white flecks"
"no more boys"
. . .
"witnesses our inadequate sex"
. . .
. . . "stone turns luminous and then returns to normal"
. . .
"attempts to summon a new boy"
. . .
"Deadboy"
. . .
"you are not involved"
. . .

"Memories resurfacing"
. . . "coagulating underneath the meniscus"
. . .
"I delay my need for glasses"
"the eye doctor . . . tells me that I can only see the past"
. . .
"slowly lifting over the crest"
. . .
"not what is happening in front of me"
. . .
"they've stopped firing rockets in the middle of the night"
. . . "it becomes difficult to project myself"
. . .
"medical time is organized into a linear model"
. . .
"smut-maker gives his body to people he does not know"
. . .
"builds an altar from cum and diorite"
. . .
"he collects these encounters"
. . .

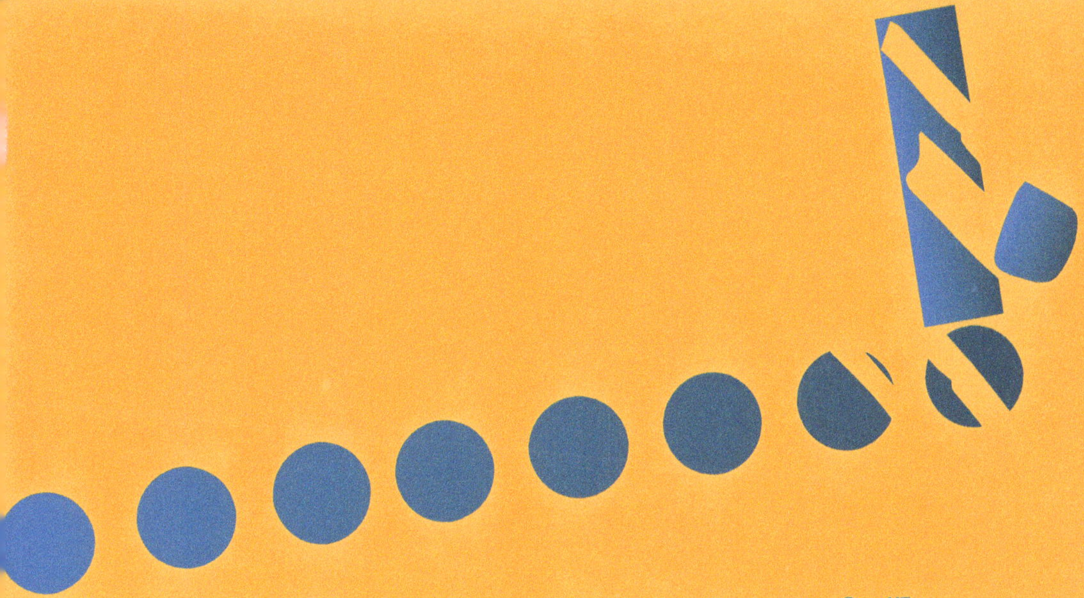

‘and feels the motivation to begin projecting again”
. .

“I am caught in the act of severing”
. . .

“somewhere north of Antwerp”
. . .

“there is no good fuck”
. . .

“he assumes that this must have meant something”
. . .

“columns of ardboard and plastic”
. . .

“Blondboy”
. . .

“it does not matter”
. . .

“the fragments will have to be assembled later”
. . .

“or in the Sonora Desert”
. . .

“rumors of defunct silos outside of Mexico City”
. . .

dilapidated in over-rowth and the slow rocess of polymer decay”
.

“replicas of the human body”
. . .

“vibrant anatomies”
. . .

“Russian operatives gift old helicopters to the Honduran government”
. . .

“extracting his self from the corporeal and bringing it somewhere else”
. . .

“the next fuck”
. . .

nother silhouette waiting over the horizon”
. . .

“in the tradition of Katrina Fritsch”
. . .

“nowhere identifiable”
. . .

“I don’t know where the path leads”
. . .

“we live in a high desert”
. . .

e timid approach delicate placement of your hands”
. . .

“Oldboy”
. . .

“smoke rises”
. . .

“Tommyboy is somewhere else now”
. . .

“Tommyboy”
. . .

“narrator-fool sleeps somewhere in the woods”
. . .

“this path is not tropical”
. . .

“they must have three or four now”
. . .

nset is green or rgundy”

“disembodied voices map the actions of a beheaded deity”
. . .

“in the shadow of someone unrecognizable.”

ACT 42

"changing the elements of your encounter"

. . .

"one segment of the greater movement-image"

. . .

"in the field of polymer reliefs and floral patterns"

. . .

"the drumset pounds"

. . .

"A young man pays his drumset outside of the metro station"

. . .

"computational errors rearranging the geography of this space"

. . .

"tongue fattening until the mouth is immobile"

. . .

"your projection is weighed down by dataplasm"

. . .

"text-
source
corrupted
by its
longevity"

. . .

**"a sun lit in
multitudes"**

. . .

"collision between bat and face."

ACT 43

"seductive

"Bolaño says that he do
to talk about his ti

"part of the greater creation myth"

"no more apologies"

"Someone in the café
tells you that everyone
here came from the same
place"

"as if their
conceptions
occurred
simultaneously"

"recorded in
undocumented gnostic
texts"

. . .

"no more
boys"

"ar
ser
proj

"a departure and
return"

. . .

. . .

"I grow distant from this place."

. . .

"each avant-gardist the offspring of a
farmer from the Yucatan"

. . .

"or his friendship with Vila-Matas in Spain"

...

"the title of a genderless and sexless creature"

...

"I do not want to go blind at a young age"

...

"or the relationship between you and him"

...

ACT 44

"daytime turns each office window into a void"

. . .

"no more boys"

. . .

"the separation between smut and the erotic"

. . .

"this erotic segmented into its unerotic segments"

. . .

"penetrated by blotches of color"

. . .

"no more static"

. . .

"debris is gathered to sculpt nude models"

. . .

"in search of lost meanings"

. . .

as if t
is closer than it us

"blooming calluses"

. . .

"000
. .

"every plan
own set of r

. . .

"00
•

"the doctor says it is normal for smaller asteroids to enter the atmosphere"

"they are not sq

"in search of a more delicate sexuality"

. . .

"they appear as they do in my projections"

. . .

. . . "it's perfectly normal for the b
out of the ordinary"

. . .

"maybe things might
come to an end"

. . .

(appl

"Projecting into a forest surrounded by tall and suspicious trees"

(applause)

. . . "he says that he lives in an apartment"

. . .

"it is a shared space"

. . .

"a family of deer"

. . .

"a pack of wolves"

"00000"

. . .

. . . "a row of teeth"

"attempts to summit the tallest building"

. . .

"Tommyboy says that he can only cum when he masturbates"

. . .

"you did not like the feeling of someone mounting themselves over your chest"

. . .

"each wall faded in the likeness of a Rothko painting"

. . .

. . .

"molded hues of color"

. . .

"smut-maker says that he does not want to be confined"

. . .

"someone scales the side of the fabricated skyline"

. . .

"his desire is intimate and not passionate"

. . .

"you recognize the architecture of this place as being past its prime."

"a musician
of Henry Du
pseudonym

. . .

"the old cop ticks his tongue like a clock"

. . .

"I
I

"0

"their prese
seems so
natural now

. . .

"dissociated fro
new landsca
. . .

ols
on
es"
. . .

its

"

s"
. .
act

"the world is not the same as it was a month ago"

. . . "white noise resting at a different frequency"

"forest organized into hallucinatory shapes"

. . .

"Beatboy sits with arced back at drumset"

. . .

"polymer acropolis dilapidated in the field of overgrowth"

. . .

"plumes of fungus and seed"

. . . "against each tightened face"

. . .

"the poet is blamed for his own death"

. . .

"mononym crawling over horizon"

. . .

"I bear witness to a self-induced hysteria"

. . .

"pools of ink or pitch"

. . . "Beatboy groaning with blooded hands"

. . .

"in which the abrasive rhythms of the music"

. . .

"a policeman fabricates new evidence on his notepad"

. . .

"lead drummer to discard sticks and begin pounding open palm"

. . .

"this gesture is both symbolic and practical"

. . . "the band begins improvising"

. . .

"have you read the Wittgenstein?"

. . .

"brass encouraging funeral march"

. . .

"I've been thinking about them all the time recently"

. . .

"vacating orifices"

. . .

"I don't know how to interpret the memories that have been resurfacing"

. . .

"my stomach rumbles unexpectedly"

. . .

"only your departure is abrupt"

. . .

"do you remember all of the names?"

. . .

"and then I am home again"

. . .

"working from the foundation of Miles Davis' Bitches Brew"

. . .

es the words
under the
nk Dumis"

"deer wander through the apartment"

. . .

not know
they first
arrived"

. . .

"scream of jazz"

. . .

"things slowly change over time"

. . .

I inherit the
id reflux of my
forbearers"

. . .

"new thoughts pour out from the sides of my head"

. . .

"you say that you cannot flourish in the lag time"

. . .

"maenads lounging"

. . .

"unedited footage ripped from dashcams"

. . .

"ooooo"

. . .

"it does not work"

. . .

"the forest a distant and elusive place"

. . .

"I attempt to project my being across time and space"

. . .

ACT 45

"creatures
constructed
from
memory"

. . .

"you cannot be
measured"

. . .

"Tom

"you have

"t
ro

"a collective of ambitious crafters further knit the chain of metaphors"

. . .

"praxis becomes finicky and unpredicta

"The band holds a
meeting where they
decide if they are a rock
band or a jazz band"

. . .

"smut-maker projects his
being onto a new plane"

. . .

"occupied
by
phantoms"

. . .

"flat facsimiles"

"Blondboy"

. . .

poy”

ension”

and of
grows
stant”
. . .

“it is only because of the dry winter”
. . .

“the stones in
your stomach
moan”
. . .

“frantic percussion echoes across
multiple timelines”
. . .

“deer rest
in clusters around
the peripheries of
the clearing”
. . .

“border between
sun and canopy”
. . .

“slow change from hues of red to red orange”
. . .

“each musician positioned atop
a different column”
. . .

“work intricate
detail into the
fractalized
metonym”
. . .

“you’re overreacting”
. . .

“this does not mean
anything”
. . .

“when I wake up my
palms are bleeding”
. . .

“narrator-fool attempts
to rebrand himself as a
somnambulist”
. . .

“someone says
something about
jouissance”
. . .

“it
does
not
work”
. . .

“he sits down and
tries to project
himself onto a
new plane”
. . .

“he tries
again and it does”
. . .

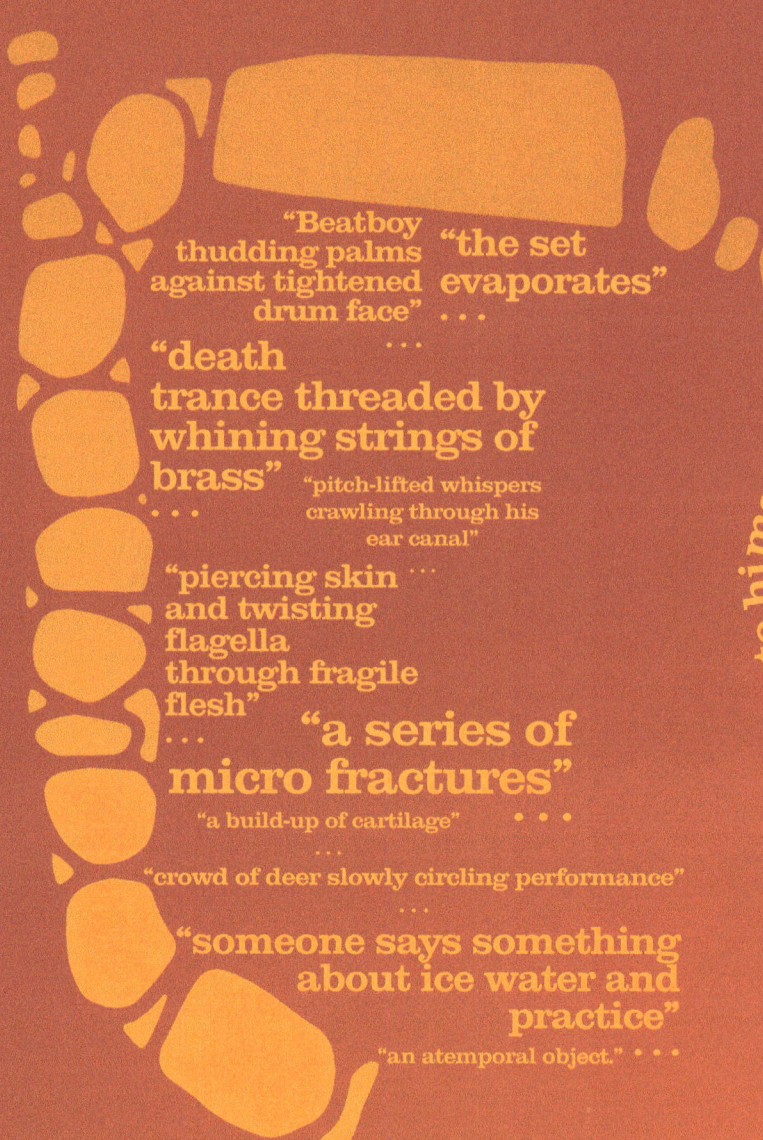

"Beatboy thudding palms against tightened drum face" . . .

"the set evaporates" . . .

. . .

"death trance threaded by whining strings of brass" . . .

"pitch-lifted whispers crawling through his ear canal" . . .

"piercing skin and twisting flagella through fragile flesh" . . .

"a series of micro fractures" . . .

"a build-up of cartilage"

. . .

"crowd of deer slowly circling performance"

. . .

"someone says something about ice water and practice"

"an atemporal object." . . .

"he attempts to separate himself from time" . . .

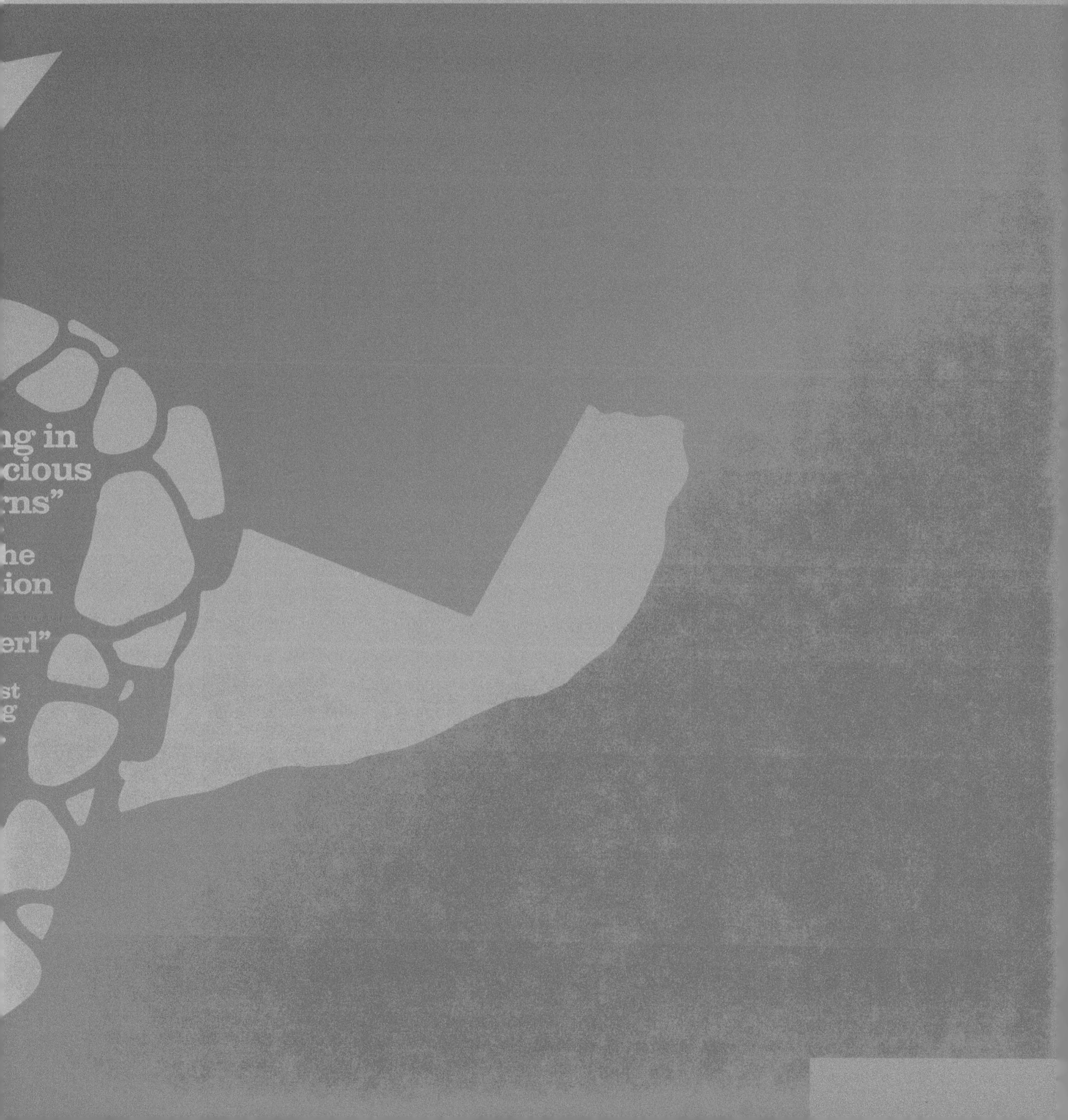
ng in
cious
rns"
he
ion
erl"
st
g

ACT 47

"smut-maker abstains from a fourth harlequin novel" "again attempting to distinguish between smut and the erotic" "findin

"I know my meat hold no miracles"

"if he was"

"there is a difference between Puritan work ethic and aimless labor"

"the unsatisfying results"

"it is animated only for a brief scene"

"and now he isn't"

"in which he treads towards an unending kind of music"

"in which I am alive and then I am not"

"rockets altering the composition of the atmosphere"

"drone not drones"

"melt into stains"

"ooooo" "your conception"

"text i

"all of my tattoos depict a hidden geometry"

"a fume of factories"

(laughter)

(laughter)

"computer vomiting keys onto the desk"

"I regret anything with people involved"

"Tommyboy said that he had to leave because the radiation was too much for him"

"I'm worried that things are exactly what I expect them to be"

"each cataclysmic moment of history the product of these interceptions"

"slow working through disparate n and mel

"Beatboy in a continued mania"

"on the sheets and duvet"

"stubbing your cigarettes by the laundry machine"

"it is radical to work without sleep or rest"

"exploratory labor"

"rain of jet fuel"

"language of an abysmal source"

"each sexual encounter that you've experienced"

ir s

"can you remember what his name was?"

"deer crowd over your ashes"

"does it matter to you anymore?"

"a speed which ha its past iterations"

"sonically hidden instructions transmitted across unlabeled radio stations"

"now that he is over and done with"

"someone says that his husband was Mexican"

"another someone asks when he stopped being Mexican"

"how n have

ferences between what is desirable and what he has made"

"sun slowly dragging over the horizon"

. . . "every assassination"

"memory of Blondboy standing outside of laundromat"

. . .

"the second is something that you say"

. . . "about a loss of substance"

. . .

"changing dawn to day to dusk"

. . .

"circumcision is the first betrayal"

"begins recruiting crew members"

. . .

"or my lessening from object to subject"

. . .

"your shirt is covered in stains"

. . .

"codes are placed in unassuming locations"

. . .

"narrator-fool admits that these desires have been integrated into the larger code."

"keys
pit from
eyboard
d scatter
mongst
rpeting"

. . .

pted with a new cipher"

. . .

lon't know the
t time I ate"

"I came to see people cum"

. . .

"in search of lost meanings"

. . .

"you say something about your desire for smut"

. . .

"Sun Ra completes the construction of his ark"

. . .

"Beatboy continuing the drone"

. . . "any dreams?"

. . .

h
hm
"

with the
n of being
led upon"

. . .

nizes with

ot know what is coming
out of my mouth"

. . .

distinct identities
ed on my tongue"

. . .

"spends the next month revisiting what has already been set in stone"

"ooooo"

. . .

"chewing on cigarette filter"

. . .

"you have no use for this information"

. . .

"they refer to her as Asterion"

. . .

"coded diagraphically in the Wittgenstein"

. . .

"someone says something about the minotaure again"

. . .

"no but I have been trying"

. . .

(laughter)

"the wooded exterior"

. . .

"not in ecology but in behavior"

. . .

"environment of anomalies and unconscious gestures"

. . .

"any memories?"

. . .

"buzzing instrumentation"

"drone not drones"

. . .

"he projects himself onto the outskirts of the city"

. . .

"landscape reminiscent of Stalker's Zone"

. . .

"drone of brass"

"I would like to go to the forest" . . . "the peripheries of the city"

. . . "not as projection but as myself" "a row of fetal structure" . . .

. . . . . .

"in which I can see first hand" "formulating the materials for an expedition"

. . . "where grand architectures are returned to infancy" . . . "bodiless claims" . . .

. . .

"pooling in sweat and blood"

. . .

"geological discrepancies realized in the ever growing layer of shit between us and the crust"

. . .

"all of t
woke a

. . . "Beat
screamin
play

"hands . . .
blistered a
raw"

. . .

"the g

. . .

nements
e" "blue cock resting large at the center of a courtyard"
. . .
"rockets slowly inching towards the upper atmosphere"
. . .
"they justify the anthropocene"
. . .
"hues of light from green to chartreuse"
. . .
"someone says something about a noise band"
. . . "that we exist simultaneously."
edpink flesh" . . .
"the sounds that you play are abrasive"
. . .
lens of Katharina Fritsch"
"says that you should listen to them"
. . .
f the smut-maker revealed in a damp and unlit room"
. . .
"in search of lost meanings"
. . .
"I do not want to speak until we are sure that one another are real"
. . .
"have you spoken with one another?"
. . .
"but information can be hard to find"
. . .

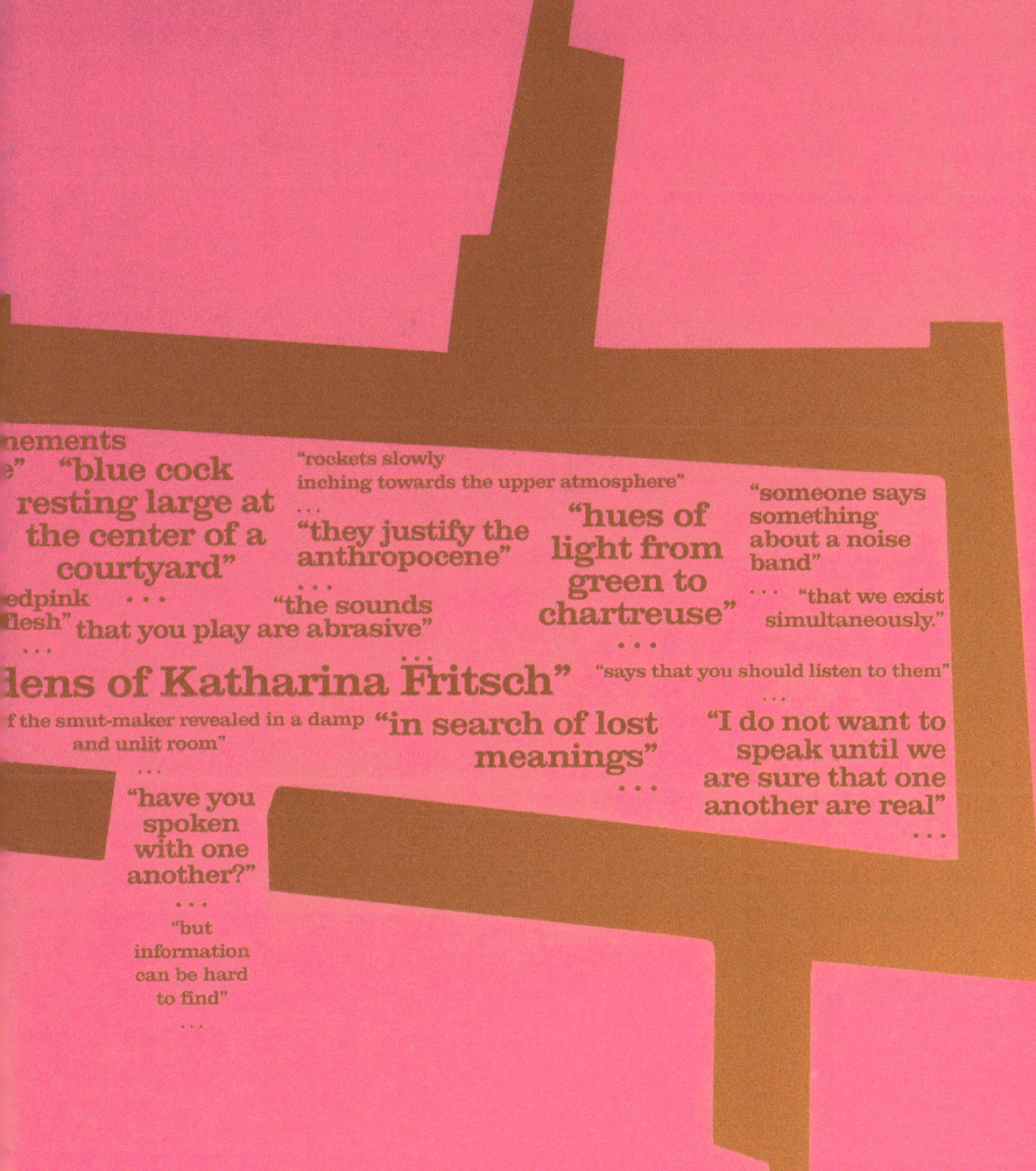

ACT 49

"I am compelled to speak" "any dreams?"

. . . "I do not have dreams"

. . .

"they are a currency I cannot justify holding onto"

. . .

. . . "smut-maker witness to a series of occult performances"

"in which the drum is animated and tortured"

. . .

"00000"

. . .

"conceived in the violence of its playing"

. . .

"I used to keep a journal of my dreams"

. . .

"but it was an expensive habit"

. . .

"and again dreams are currency"

. . . "00000" "a row of teeth"

. . .

"Beatboy slowly begins appearing closer to uptown"

. . .

"witness to the aging towers"

. . .

"but assumes that it must be someone else"

. . .

"nothing lost"

. . .

"in a more active position than myself"

. . .

"journeying into the unfamiliar density"

. . .

"they attempt to leave a note behind"

. . .

"someone says something about mythopoeia"

. . .

"a certain image is projected onto the cityscape"

. . .

"I do not know how to describe it"

. . .

"I have trouble forming the entirety of a word"

. . .

"flirtations misconstrued as a failure to enunciate"

. . .

"nothing shared"
. . .

"placeholder title"
. . .

"the genderless sexless organism"
. . .

"there is no one left for me to desire"
. . .

"Beatboy an anomaly of this new era"
. . .

"I feel an affiliation"
. . .

"I am told that I mutter when I talk to people"
. . .

"but it does not add up"
. . .

"but you refuse to take it."

"towers of cardboard lift from their foundation"

"garden of polymer"
. . .

"vibrant statues luminous at night"
. . .

"I'd rather just not know what I'm looking at"
. . .

"no more boys"
. . .

"on more important endeavours"
. . .

"electricity crawls along the wire"
. . .

"it is easier to dismiss what you cannot see"
. . .

"a rising hum"
. . .

"this is not a moment worth revisiting"
. . .

"the wall is pressed with newly printed wallpapers"
. . .

"they should be spent elsewhere"
. . .

"new exhibits are installed at the museum"
. . .

"00000"
. . .

"if you squint you can't even see it"
. . .

"applied to the surface with restoration grade adhesives"
. . .

"someone mentions an avant-garde photographer"
. . .

"narrator-fool is told a rumor about Blondboy"
. . .

"amassing crowds and structures"
. . .

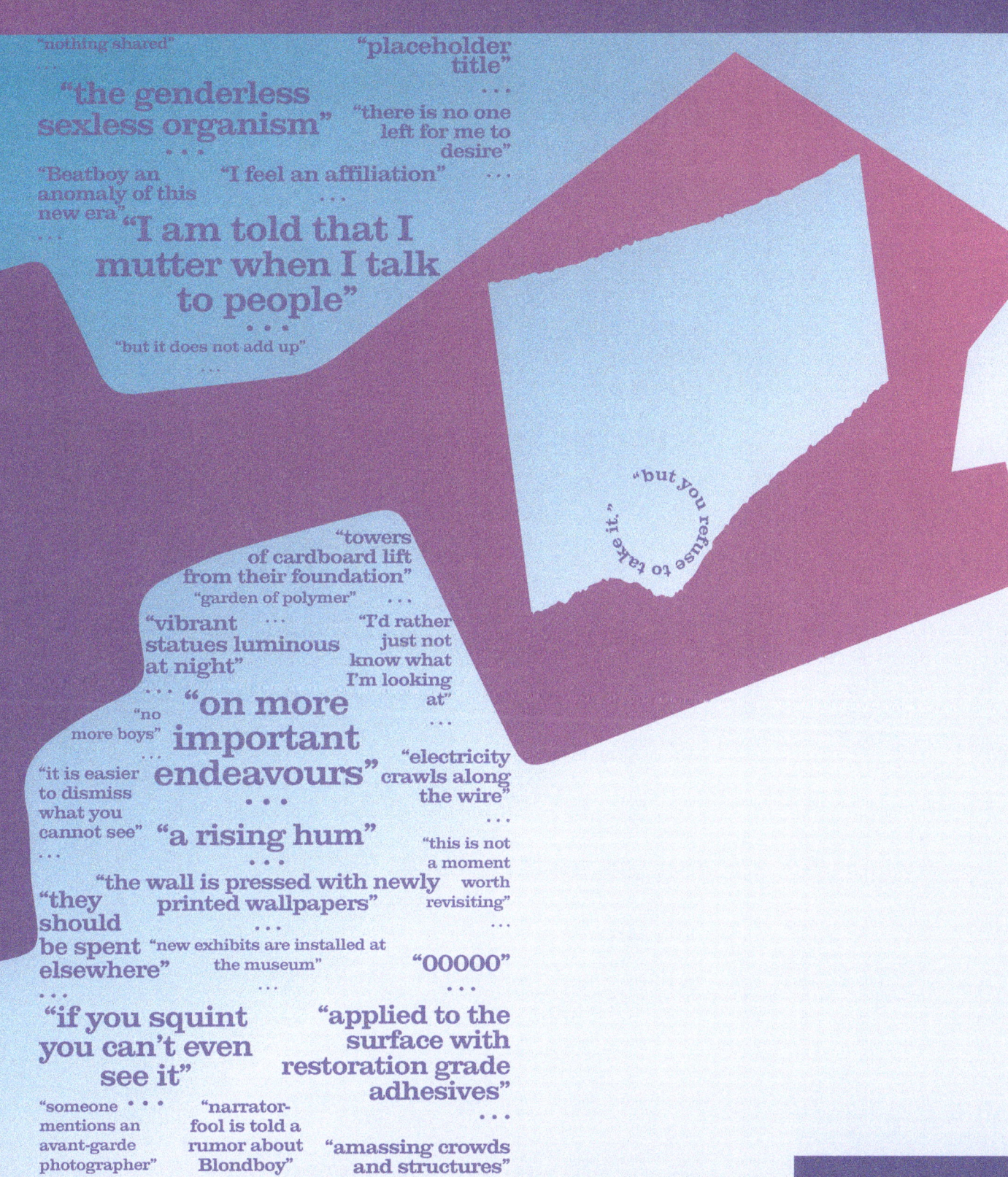

ACT 50

"I am given a handful of dirt"

. . .

"each new iteration of the text is rendered tactile"

. . .

"I continue to dictate"

. . .

"hand moving across surface"

. . . "the eye doctor tells me that I can only see what has been spoken of"

. . .

"blackblood pools on the ground"

. . .

"my skull is emptied of its contents"

. . .

"in search of lost meanings"

. . .

"where each step reforms the original swell"

. . .

"column of instrumentalists"

. . .

"slouching towards a new dreamscape."

. . . "my mouth cannot close"

"langu

"Beatboy resting somewhere between corporeal and spectral" . . .

"I have the desire to stop but I am refused" . . .

"an apparition with tangible flesh" . . .

"it absorbs into the carpet" . . .

"nature shifting from green to turquoise" . . .

"moss film burrowing into my pores" . . .

"spreading from each arborescent source" . . .

"your response haptic and pleased" . . .

"real people live in cities" . . .

"old cop writes himself a note about the difference between collisions and accidents" . . .

"video footage ripped from a larger archive" . . .

festering in the caves of bloody mouth and eyes world" . . .

ACT 51

"this inte
devolving into a m
series of ap

"Above us
there is a vacuum devoid of
material"
. . .

"00000"
. . .
"by the digital speech of nighttime rockets"
. . .

"a continuous jazz"
. . .

"I feel emboldened by
nuclear language"
. . .

"smut-maker saying something
about"
. . .

"Beatboy plays until his
hands are numb"
. . .

"and he can no longer control
his technique"
. . .

"inchi
"fueled by drone of drum"
. . .

"wading
through jet
fuel and
rain"
. . .

"reasonable people and unreasonable people"
. . .

"unending music"
. . .

“improvised
funeral march”
. . .

tion
ered
gies”
. . .

“dirt clings
to your
skin”
. . .

“or about unreasonable
people and unreasonable
people”
. . .

“ooooo”
. . .

“garden of plastic
facsimiles”
. . .

“Bolaño
sits down
with Mike Corrao
under the pretense of
coffee”
. . .

towards self-
destruction.”

ACT 52

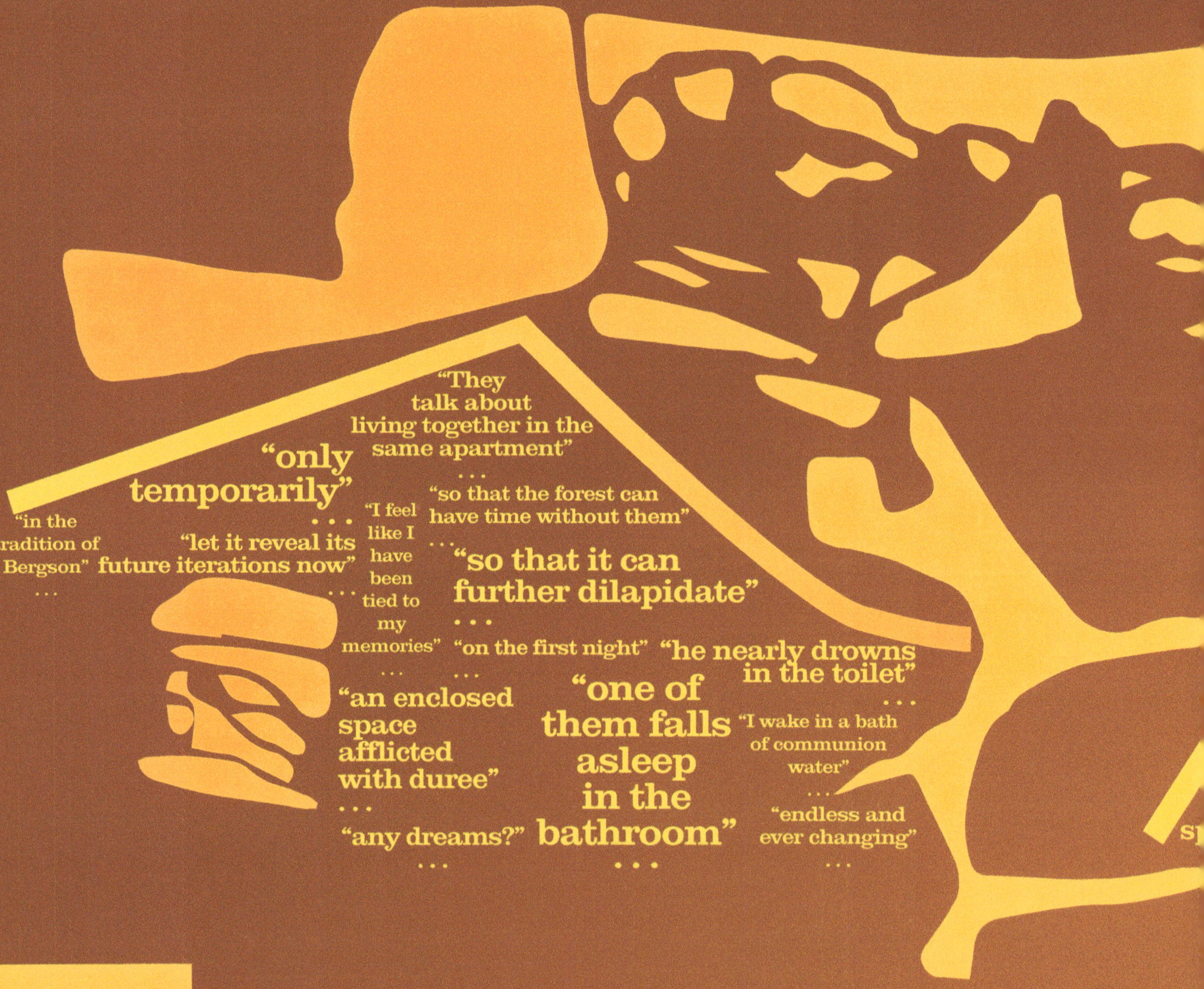
"They talk about living together in the same apartment"
. . .
"only temporarily"
. . .
"in the tradition of Bergson"
. . .
"let it reveal its future iterations now"
. . .
"I feel like I have been tied to my memories"
. . .
"so that the forest can have time without them"
. . .
"so that it can further dilapidate"
. . .
"on the first night"
. . .
"he nearly drowns in the toilet"
. . .
"an enclosed space afflicted with duree"
. . .
"one of them falls asleep in the bathroom"
. . .
"I wake in a bath of communion water"
. . .
"endless and ever changing"
. . .
"any dreams?"
. . .

“blood coagulates along my arms and legs”

. . .

“limbs tangled between sheets and duvet”

. . .

“00000”

. . .

“space is ade from s of black nd white”

. . . . .

“this does not mean anything”

. . .

“with the desire to undo some larger and more complicated knot”

. . .

“it is not what I intended”

. . .

“you're gonna carry that weight”

. . .

“the manifestation of something divine”

. . .

“sun mutating into a new shape”

. . .

“00000”

. . .

“a collective of ambitious architectures reorients the underground segments of the city”

. . .

“weaving them in rhizomatic patterns”

. . .

“each tunnel broken down into its immobile segments”

. . .

“this is not what I want”

. . .

“now is a time of refused isolation.”

ACT 53

"subtle feature of the greater mise-en-scene" . . .

"writes a prescription for kino eye" . . .

"or a prescription for the more recent" . . .

"the initial becoming"
. . .

"even if our feelings are not mutual"
. . .

"its inevitability becomes more familiar"
. . .

"says that it is haunting but beneficial"
. . .

"the eye doctor says that I am oblivious to my surroundings"
. . .

"then death is made less tragic"
. . .

"and I think this is okay"
. . .

"if everyone has begun to die"
. . .

"Narrator-fool begins the process of review"
. . .

"connecting each disparate image in his repertoire"
. . .

"looking for some kind of through line"
. . .

"a pair of academics ask for a more thorough definition of the schizopastoral"
. . .

"an email arrives"
. . .

"you say that you are not affiliated"
. . .

"this is not your word"
. . .

"language is broken down into each facet of its use"
. . .

"the chain and the fractal"
. . .

"language-image"
. . .

"broken down into its non-linguistic segments"
. . .

"when is the last time that you masturbated?"
. . .

"I cannot sleep"
. . .

"the poor image"
. . .

"your body a collection of cut-ups from after you shot your boywife"
. . .

"the sheets are malleable"
. . .

"becoming-papier-mache"
. . .

"in spite of Adorno"
. . .

"you are not affiliated with the voices pouring from my mouth"
. . .

"blood let"
. . .

"their pre-corpse lounging in an unassuming position"
. . .

"hold on"
. . .

"my posture evidence of naiveté"
. . .

"jazz permeating"
. . .

"which I upload"
. . .

"the f[...] e[...]

"is only soft evidence"
. . .

"the fact that you [...] alive"
. . .

"flecks of fat or cartilage"
. . .

kn[...]

"muscles separated i[...] their distinct fibre[...]
. . .

"face of sandpap[...] grinding against thigh"
. . .

"revealing flesh or bone"
. . .

"in the tradition of myself[...]
. . .

"or if the wei[...]

"matriarch interrupts scene by performing a virgin birth"
. . .

"says that this is not proof of her purity"
. . .

"but her refusal to participate in something she does not want to be associated with"
. . .

"I am okay with this."

"two flights arrive in Santiago"
. . .

"he does not want to have sex with anyone"
. . .

"passengers enact a melodrama"
. . .

"Beatboy says he does not want to have sex with me"
. . .

"parents shaped from minor constellations"
. . .

"Orion towering over your lineage"
. . .

"three murders are discovered and solved"
. . .

"ooooo"
. . .

"mockingly"
. . .

(applause)

"last night the rockets were already far away"
. . .

"specks of dust in the upper atmosphere"
. . .

"whether or not they are trying to have sex"
. . .

"it is in the blood"
. . .

"smut-maker circles his previous novels like they are cursed artifacts"
. . .

"memory of Blondboy moving out yesterday"
. . .

"carried with you on departure from the womb"
. . .

"we have not tried to"
. . .

"we have not done anything"
. . .

compressed beyond usability"
. . .

"each missile is followed by an orange crescent"
. . .

"I'm thinking"
. . .

age of our
unter"
. .

"coded so that I am the only one aware of its contents"
. . .

"narrator-fool attempts to map his relationship to Beatboy"
. . .

"in the shift from fetus to human"
. . .

"Wittgenstein lingering in the unfocused background"
. . .

till

e key my
ge of who
you are"
. . .

"Ginsberg is resurrected"
. . .

"and then returned to death"
. . .

"or if one of them is just being polite"
. . .

"the Kaddish experiences a brief revival as well"
. . .

"from ashen frame"
. . .

"and what you really look like"
. .

"it does not matter"
. . .

"or if they have decided yet"
. . .

er

ut-maker vomits
he shower"

"kino brush"
. . .

of former fuck-ups is unethical to hand off to someone else"
. . .

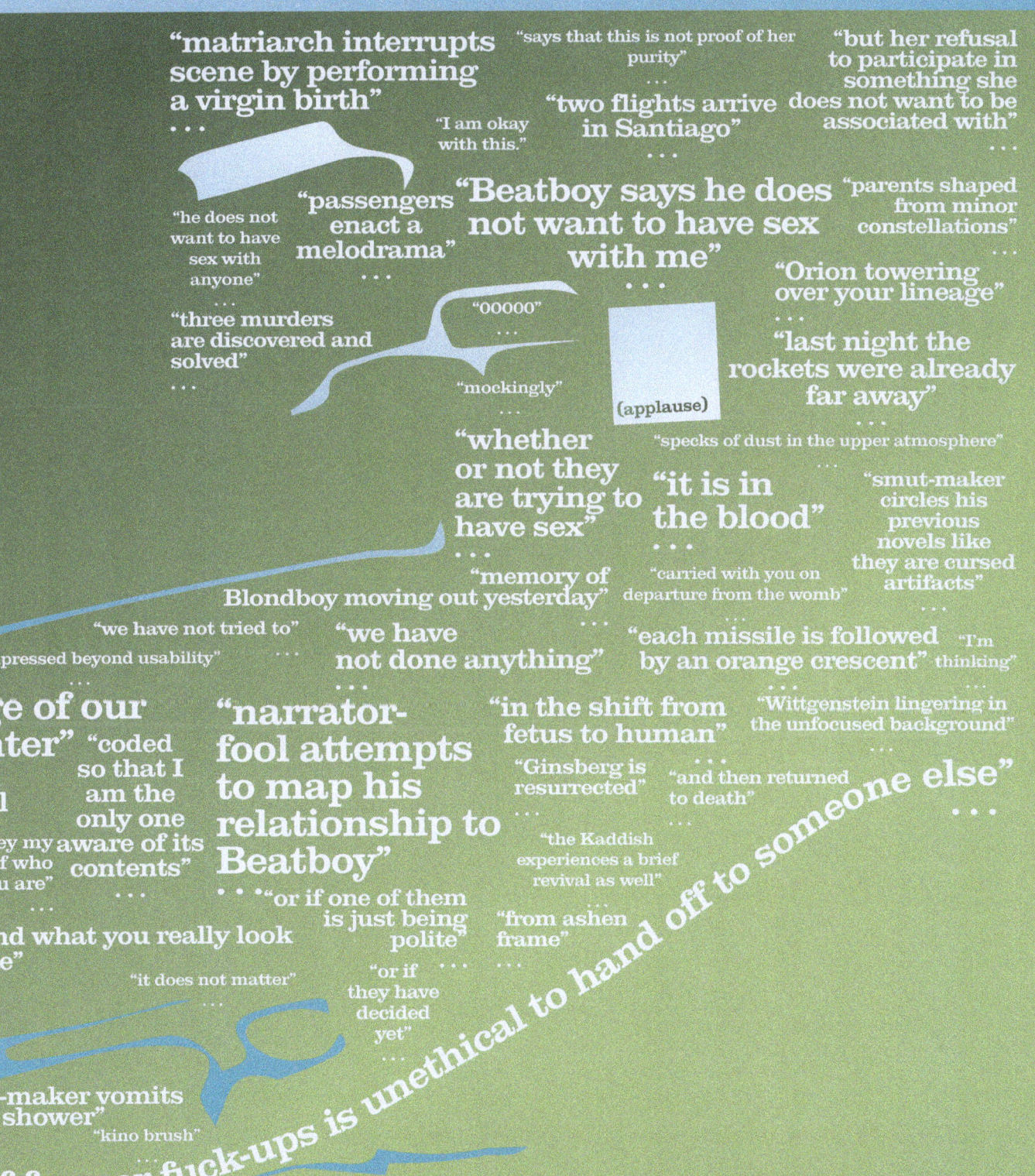

ACT 54

"an altar is constructed
twigs and soaps

"jet fuel dissipates
into a sheet of
mist"
. . .

"Mike Corr
performs a
which ends
dry heavin
the surface
. . .

"but his methods lose their h
qualities"
. . .

"the
boon an object"
. . .

"he suffers a withdrawal
from the garden"
. . .

"attempts
to play"
. . .

"we are
here
now"
. . .

"hue shifting
in random
intervals"
. . .

"but
not in the
tradition of Proust"
. . .

"drones not
drone"
. . .

"the sunset
is made from
amateurly mixed
paint"
. . .

"coats
the skin
of the
subject"
. . .

"with a dream-
like pace"
. . .

scal year."
. . .

"Every problem thus
far has been a figment of the imagination"
. . .

"Beatboy says
that he cannot
pay his rent"
. . .

"if the moon is
late that means
something"
. . .

"in search of
lost meanings"
. . .

"there is
something
more tactile at
hand"
. . .

"or it
comes up
too early"
. . .

"in the
tradition of
Weerasethakul"
. . .

"buzzing
overhead"
. . .

"sometimes the
moon does not
come up at all"
. . .

"bar

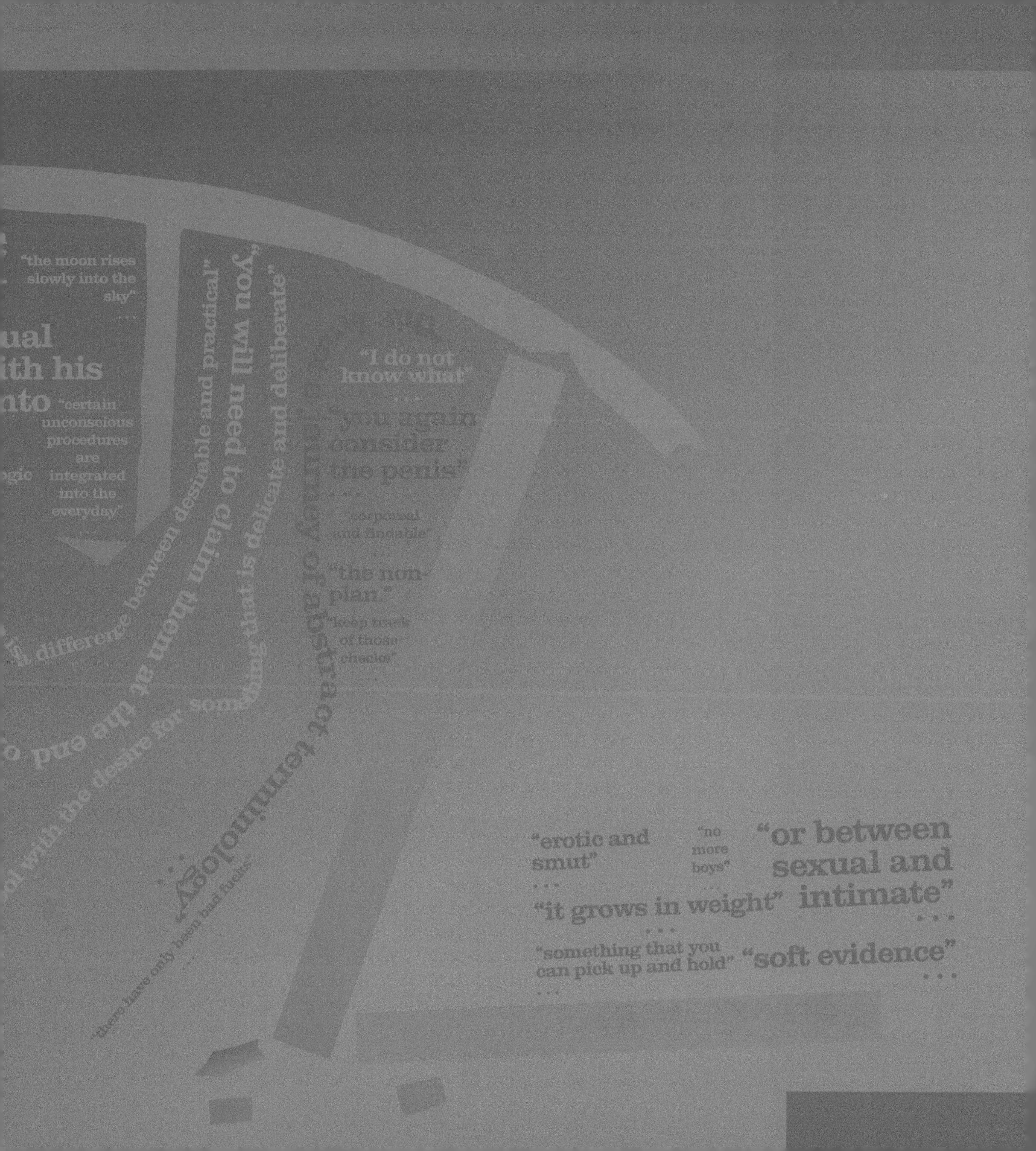
"the moon rises slowly into the sky"
. . .
ual
ith his
nto
"certain unconscious procedures are integrated into the everyday"
ogic
difference between desirable and practical"
"you will need to claim them at the end o
"something that is delicate and deliberate"
ol with the desire for some
"I do not know what"
. . .
"you again consider the penis"
. . .
"corporeal and fingable"
"the non-plan."
"keep track of those checks"
abstract terminology
"there have only been bad fucks"
"erotic and smut"
. . .
"no more boys"
"or between sexual and intimate"
. . .
"it grows in weight"
. . .
"something that you can pick up and hold"
. . .
"soft evidence"
. . .

ACT 55

"whatever misinterpretations have happen

"Do you serve coffee here?"
. . .

"but still"
. . .

"just black coffee"
. . .

"are the cups plastic or paper?"

"Bolaño ambivalent about this conversation"
. . .

"more that it is happening again for the umpteenth time"

. . .

"without cream or sugar"

"I cannot recognize your face"
. . .

. . .

"and that no progress has been made"
. . .

"and . . . that the problem itself has yet to be spoken of"
. . .

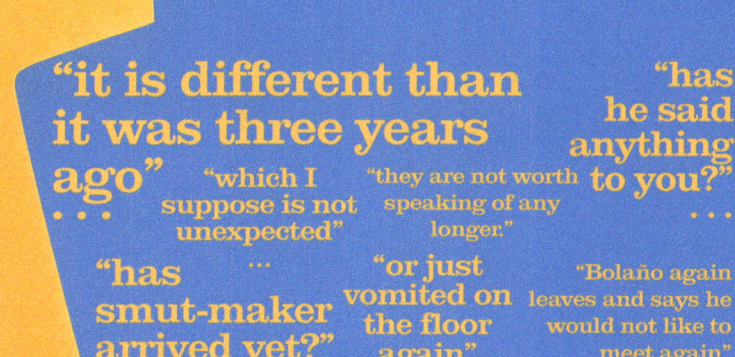

"it is different than it was three years ago"
. . .

"which I suppose is not unexpected"
. . .

"they are not worth speaking of any longer."

"has he said anything to you?"
. . .

"has smut-maker arrived yet?"
. . .

"or just vomited on the floor again"
. . .

"Bolaño again leaves and says he would not like to meet again"
. . .

ACT 56

"The doctor decides that it is not important to distinguish between stigmata and astigmatism"

"trilogy of failed encounters"

"it is emptied of people" . . .

"it is shrouded by overgrowth" . . .

. . . **"palms and eyes dripping clumps of blood"**

"narrator-fool attempts to enter Blondboy" . . .

. . . **"silhouette carrying bags of sand over his shoulder"** . . .

"memory of Tommyboy saying that he could only cum when he masturbated" . . .

"I do not know if I need glasses or intervention" . . .

"but this is not how astral projection is done" . . .

"not everybody is going to want to fuck you" . . .

"polymer acropolis remains" . . .

. . . "three exorcists perform an archaic ritual" . . .

"crimson slog" . . .

"King Lear is killed by his own paranoia" . . .

"this is the nature of your existence" . . .

"but now in a more hidden state" . . .

"it is n

"my vision remains unreliable"

"drums have yet to drone" . . .

"it is something to be thankful for" . . .

"the drummer asks you wha you saw" . . .

"it :

. . . **"head and hands subject to chronic soreness"**

"smut-maker projects his being into the forest again" . . .

"incapable of decomposing" . . .

. . . "

"this collage directly collected from my mouth" . . .

"on another plane" . . .

"scum of the earth" . . .

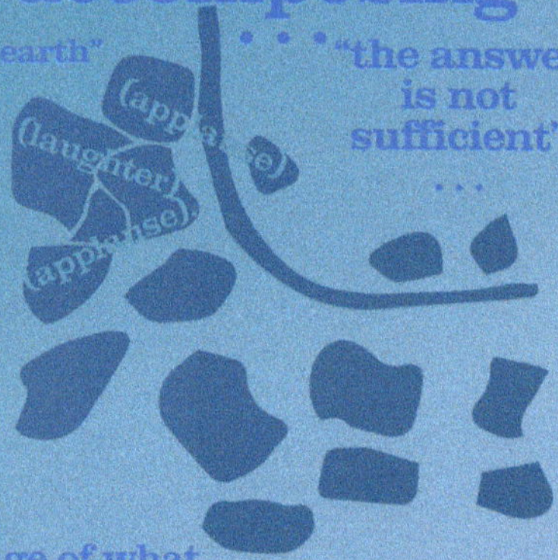

"the answer is not sufficient" . . .

. . . **"someone asks how Beatboy has been doing?"** . . .

"drone not drones" . . .

"avant-gardists dwindling" . . .

"stranger outside of laundromat with paper cup" . . .

"the orphic desire to see what you should not see" . . .

"I do not want to fuck your drums" . . .

"your sex an excuse to expand his practices" . . .

"the fourth a refusal to continue" . . .

"you could go there and come right back" . . .

"00000" . . .

"because you love it" . . .

"a collage of what the deliberate and delicate" . . .

"Tommyboy . . .

"I am not surprised" . . .

"or he cannot bear the full length of this duration" . . .

"and sometimes love is nothing but morbid curiosity" . . .

"fragile erotic gestures" . . .

"drinking coffee and then stuffing the crushed cup into their pocket" . . .

"you are pained by your desire remain reclusive" . . .

"a crowd of strangers" . . .

"in contrast to each of the three harlequin novels" . . .

"Beatboy says that he is returning to the garden son" . . .

"in another dimension" . . .

"to masturbate with other people" . . .

"using you as a totem or image" . . .

"I am not" . . .

"Beatboy" . . .

"Beatboy says that he has to leave soon" . . .

"a mission of Jesuits" . . .

"Blondboy" . . .

"enough time has passed" . . .

…ere do you start when the task is reconstruction?"
. . .

"astral projection is an unhealthy solution to a long term issue"
. . .

"three …ecutions at …igh noon"
. . .

…tive and paranoid"
. . .

…n issue"
. . .

…non-issue"

…s some kind of ethical code that prevents our meeting"

…e . . .

"my identity is separate from every other smut-maker"
. . .

"nothing that I can remember"
. . .

"what are you running from?"
. . .

"you need to be more fiscally responsible"
. . .

"Beatboy does not want to have sex with me and this is okay"
. . .

"how many voices do I contain?"
. . .

"the sun becomes a color that it should not be"
. . .

"as a new mimetic cinema"
. . .

"jaunting across the Sonora desert"
. . .

"smugglers are intercepted during their border crossing"
. . .

"but our closeness is not okay"
. . .

…r roam through the …opy and into the clearing"

"interrogation techniques are amoral but undocumented"
. . .

…not know how to verbalize it"

…is not something we …ould get used to"

"any dreams?"
. . .

"succulent are planted in the sink and on the windowsill"
. . .

"if there infinite dimensions then there is one where you have found a healthier alternative"
. . .

"the kitchen is split between two residents"
. . .

"any memories?"
. . .

"smut-maker falls asleep in an empty bathtub"
. . .

"each iteration is sentient and malleable"
. . .

"one part of the larger collage"
. . .

"but fragile in this dishonesty"
. . .

"00000"
. . .

"I do not control every other myself"
. . .

"it is an assemblage of red and blue and yellow"
. . .

"pixels in the tradition of Seurat"
. . .

"memories further complexifying"
. . .

"when I am close I can see what is true"
. . .

"dishonest in their facade"
. . .

"but I do not want to stand so close"
. . .

"00000"
. . .

"I do not know if I want to have sex or if I would just like to witness it"
. . .

"a change in identities"
. . .

"I do not know if I want to have sex with him either"
. . .

"when I close my eyes the fur of the static remains"
. . .

"familiar in its illness"
. . .

"my head feels so disjointed"
. . .

"converting static into a singular image"
. . .

"and suffer the radiation"
. . .

"where black is not black"
. . .

ACT 57

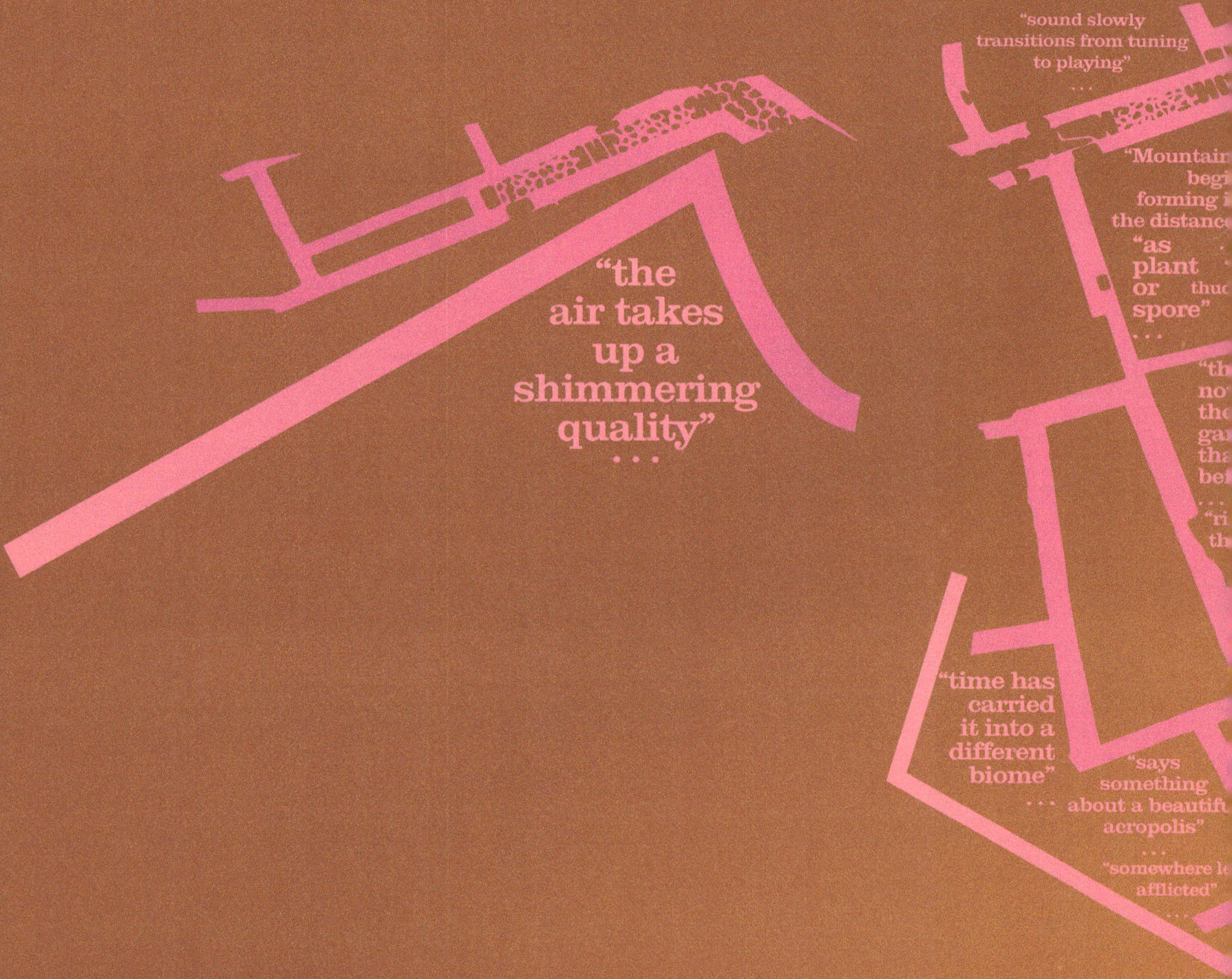
“sound slowly transitions from tuning to playing”
. . .
“the air takes up a shimmering quality”
. . .
“as plant or spore”
. . .
“time has carried it into a different biome”
. . .
“says something about a beautiful acropolis”
. . .
afflicted”
. . .

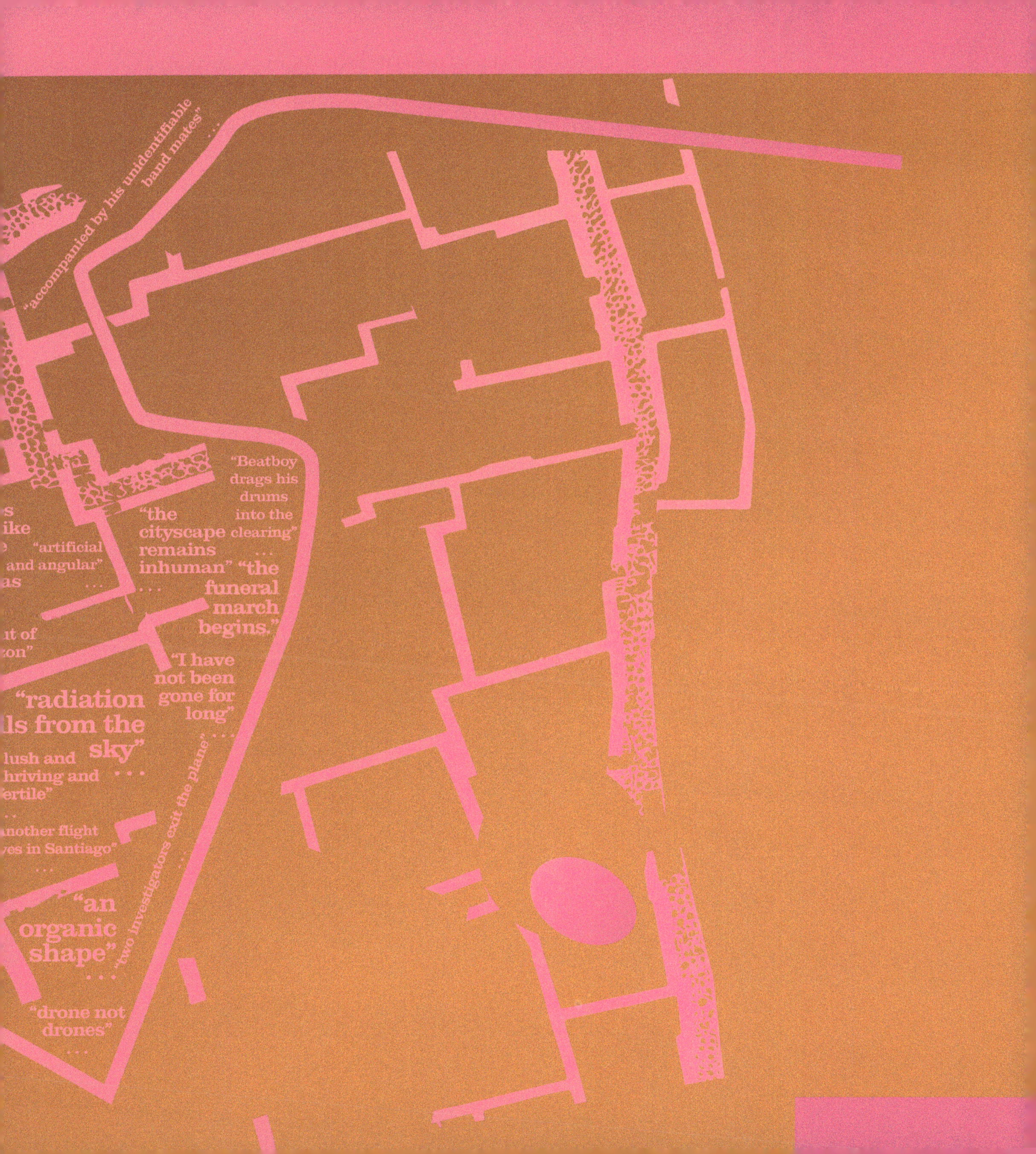
"accompanied by his unidentifiable band mates" . . .
"Beatboy drags his drums into the clearing" . . .
"the cityscape remains inhuman" . . .
"artificial and angular" . . .
"the funeral march begins."
"I have not been gone for long" . . .
"radiation
lls from the sky" . . .
lush and
hriving and
fertile"
another flight
ves in Santiago" . . .
"two investigators exit the plane" . . .
"an organic shape" . . .
"drone not drones" . . .

ACT 58

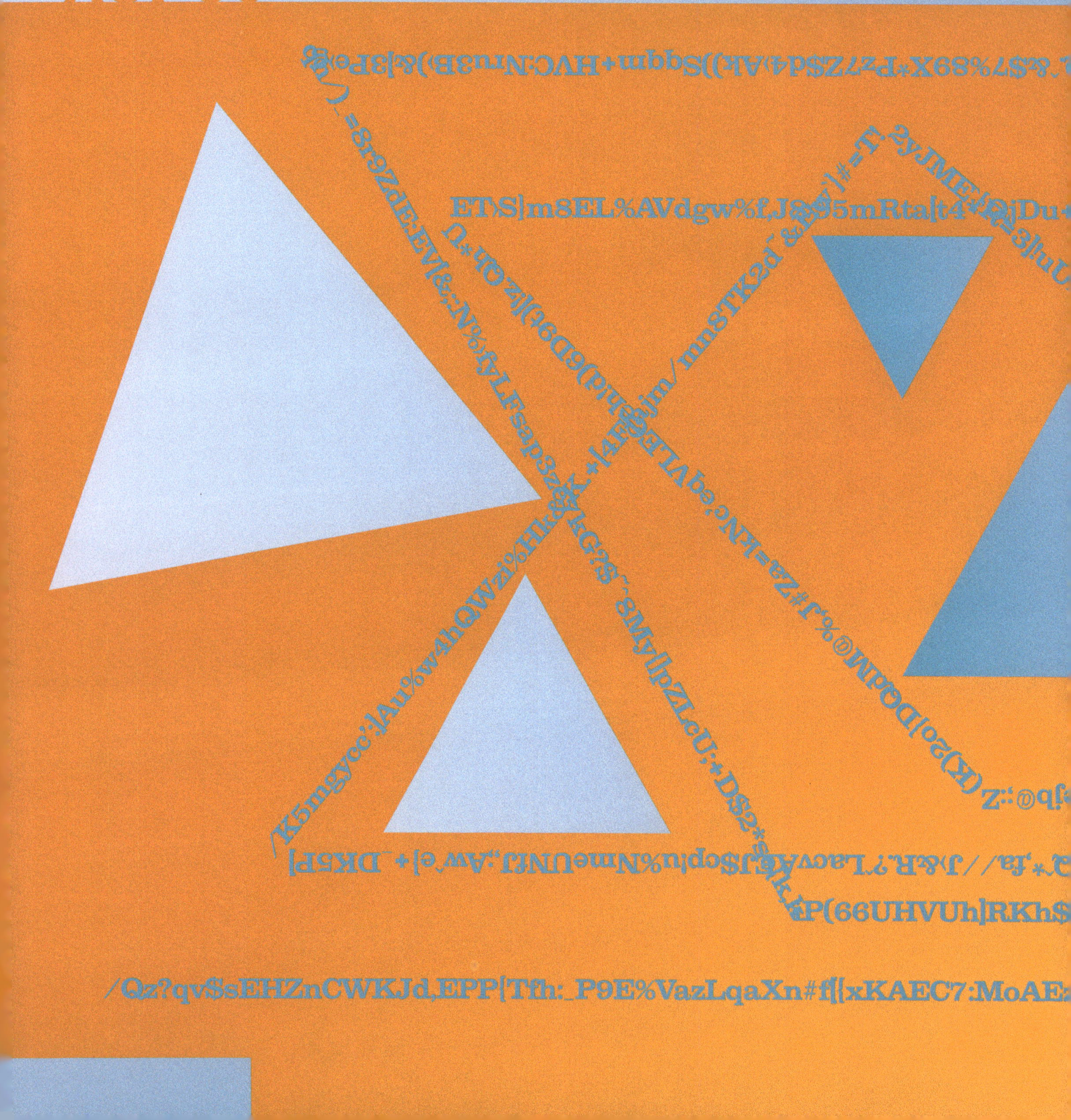

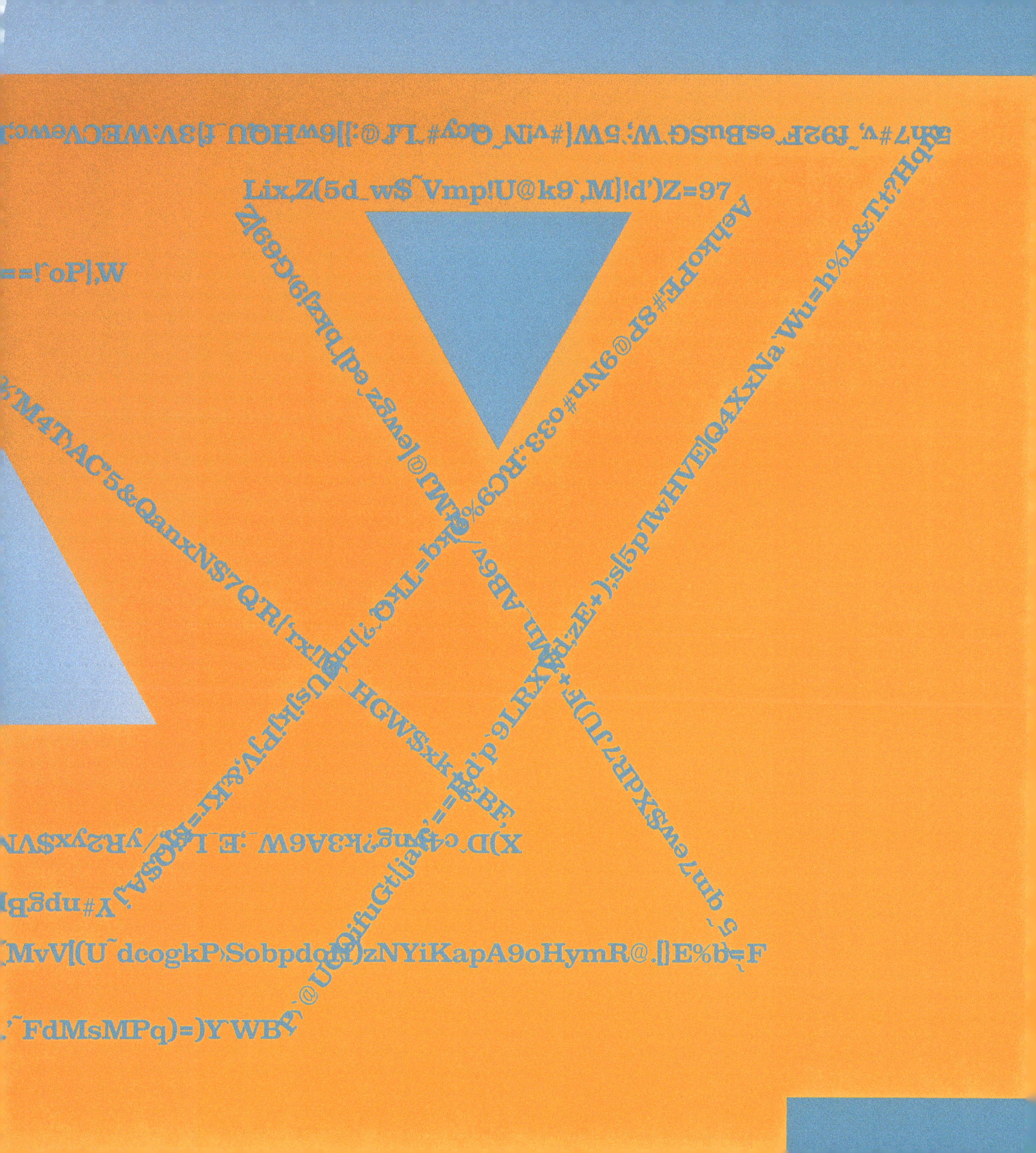
Lix,Z(5d_w$˜Vmp!U@k9`,M]!d')Z=97
==!`oP],W
(MvV](U˜dcogkP›Sobpdo
)zNYiKapA9oHymR@.[]E%b=F
.˜FdMsMPq)=)YWB

(laughter)

"Wait"

. . .

"the overproduction of language"

. . .

"flinching at each pop"

. . .

"~~as an endless stream of voices rise~~"

. . .

"I have seen this before"

. . .

"I do not know what he is talking about"

. . .

"let's begin again"

. . .

"00000"

. . .

"godhead testing the TMJ of its jaw"

. . .

"the being of all being"

. . .

"~~our mouth is left~~ ajar"

. . .

"00000"

. . .

"~~through our throat and flood the room~~"

. . .

"hi
sch
loi
ou
ba
. . .

"d

now
no
any

"s
m
yo
. . .

ers
g
of a
Tommyboy" "what is this?"

. . .

lling populations"

. . .

dification of the ocean"

. . .

"but in our
migration
to the
digital
badlands"

. . .

s "an arrival
o from outer space"

. . .

rate from the
tic cinema of
lesires"

. . . "you
consider a cinema
of the interface"

. . .

"excitations forming in the wave"

. . .

"it might take on
a new meaning"

. . .

"glitches in
the larger
infrastructure"

. . .

"a stranger head-butts me until
my skull has begun to cave in"

. . .

"someone says something about
playing on their phone"

. . . "Blondboy"

. . .

"Freudian
in their pseudointellectual
prowess"

. . .

"gray matter
shapes itself
around new
crater"

. . .

"I do not know"

. . .

"what
time is
it?"

. . .

"Beatboy"

. . .

"smut-maker weeps with
either joy or sadness"

. . .

"this
is a
miracle"

. . .

"it is good that he left"

. . .

"we think"

. . .

"yonic and phallic image
remain insufficient"

. . . "hurry up please
it's time to go"

. . .

"this
is
sabotage"

. . .

"every
clock
has been
destroyed"

. . .

"I want to be a good person."

ACT 60

ACT 61

"I close my eyes."

"or decaying paint"
. . .

"I cannot find myself in the text"
. . .

"in the thudding of the drum kit"
. . .

"it is lost on me now"
. . .

"into the ground water"
. . .

"I consume the remnants of a paranoid dream"
. . .

"and again the same miscommunication happens"
. . .

~~"our mouth is left ajar"~~
. . .

"Mike Corrao refuses to eat until Bolaño says that they can meet again"
. . .

"jet fuetl floats onto the surface"
. . .

"one more time"
. . .

"each new paragraph a

"air and not air"
. . .

"drips through soil"
. . .

"nourished by irradiated minerals"
. . .

"at the junction between space and earth"
. . .

~~"as an endless stream of voices rise"~~
. . .

"rockets resting at the crest of the planet"
. . .

"no reason for me to get glasses"
. . .

"what time is it?"
. . .

"Let's begin again"
. . .

"no reason for smut-maker to get glasses"
. . .

"there was no reason for you to get glasses"
. . .

"glitchscape of white noise"
. . .

~~"through our throat and flood the room"~~
. . .

"is this just a myth?"
. . .

"no reason for narrator-fool to get glasses"
. . .

"could you see before all of this?"
. . .

"I am described as never having read the Wittgenstein"
. . .

"he says he was
raised in the north
of Mexico"
. . .

"a product
of vomitus
praxis"
. . .

"the overproduction of meaning"
. . .

"it is documented
as incomplete and
conspiratorial"
. . .

"the schizopastoral
is brought into
question"
. . .

"smut-maker performs vomitus
praxis and creates this"
. . .

"the sound of mechanical
activity"
. . .

"let's begin again"
. . .

"an apology and a question about what is
being apologized for"
. . .

ttering of ink blotches"

"energy that is artificial and kinetic"
. . .

"as an endless
stream of
voices rise"
. . .

"text in the
tradition of
Rothko"
. . .

"materials reveal themselves to be limited"
. . .

"through our throat and
flood the room"
. . .

"silhouette stubs
cigarette and
takes another
drag"
. . .

"our
mouth is
left ajar"
. . .

"Donald Judd
mentions a
fascination
with
television
and fixed
lighting"
. . .

"language
recycles from one
arrangement to
the next"
. . .

"this recycling
an essential
component of the
greater rhythm"
. . .

"what
you are
reading"
. . .

"voices flow from a singular source"
. . .

ACT 62

E`{R=3]!uU/j(/Qz?qv$

HZnCWKJd,EPP{Tfh:_P9E%Vaz

ACT 63

"I cannot remember"
. . .

"books are stolen from the shelf in my apartment"
. . .

"strangers loitering outside of my apartment"
. . .

"Blondboy"
. . .

"everything is red or orange"
. . .

"and act with its own volition"
. . .

"my body begins to betray me"
. . .

"an a
artifi
. . .

"Tommyboy"
. . .

"Beatboy"
. . .

"Raining jet fuel ignites the forest"
. . .

"but I

"the construction incomplete without the inclusion of the body"
. . .

"helios
drags
new
fake sun
across
scalp of
forest"
. . .

"in which ea

“I know where the path leads.”

“cut from the original
name-source”

. . .

“Sun Ra continues to recruit crew members for his ark”

. . .

“the laundromat says that it does not have any vacant machines right now”

. . .

“each name divides into smaller names”

. . .

“someone says something about the
minotaure and you break their jaw
before they can finish”

. . .

“I do not know how yet”

. . .

pt to replace the sunset with an
epresentation”

that it is onset”

. . .

per noun has
derived from”

. . .

ACT 64

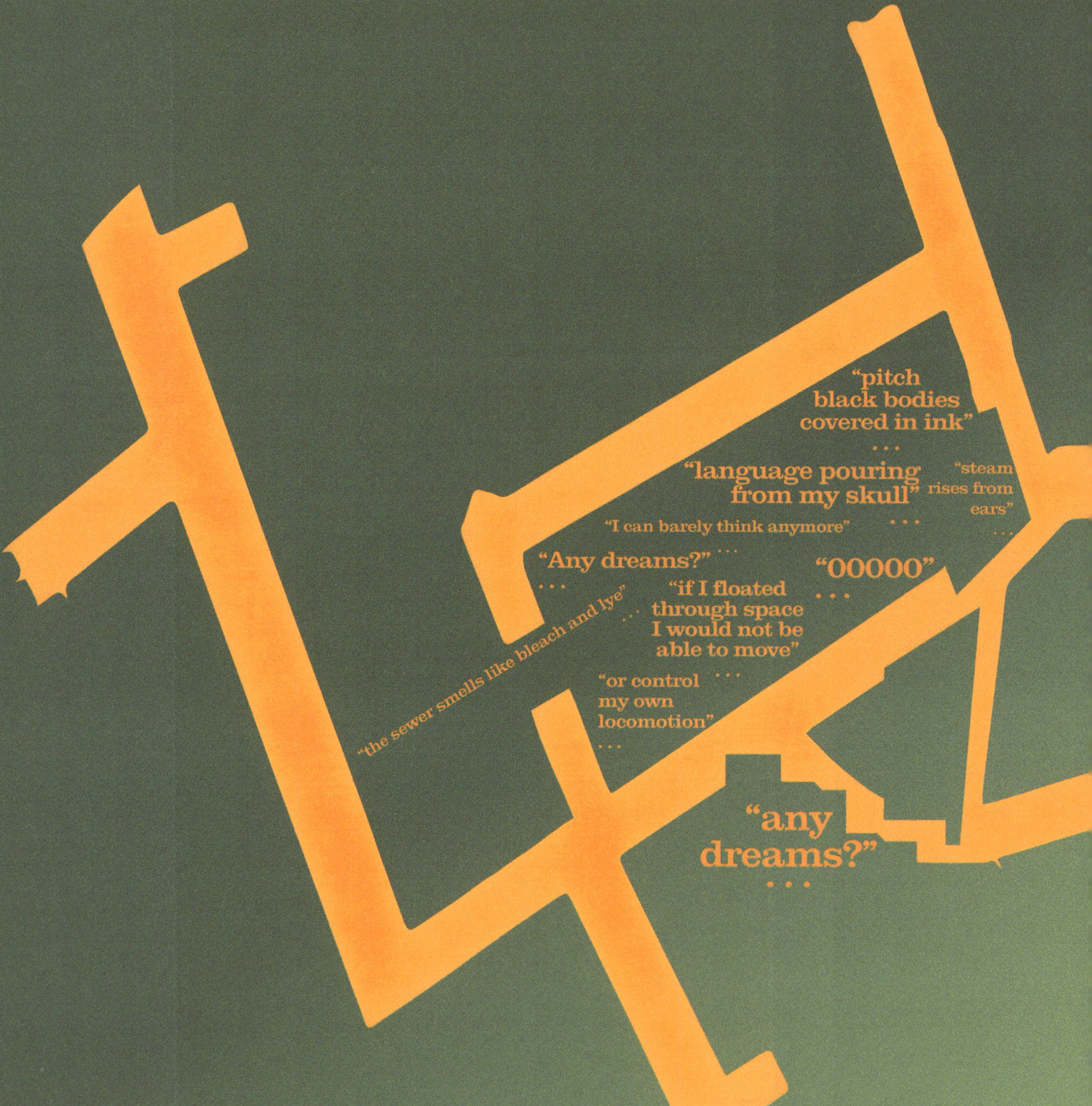
"pitch black bodies covered in ink"
. . .
"language pouring from my skull"
. . .
"steam rises from ears"
. . .
"I can barely think anymore"
. . .
"Any dreams?"
. . .
"OOOOO"
. . .
"if I floated through space I would not be able to move"
. . .
"the sewer smells like bleach and lye"
. . .
"or control my own locomotion"
. . .
"any dreams?"
. . .

“we don’t associate with one another anymore.”

“they condense on the leaves and drip back onto the concrete”

. . .

“morphemes tested on an improvised tongue”

. . .

“body attempting to regular its homeostasis”

. . .

“none of my dreams have returned”

. . .

“I woke up in the middle of the night with stomach pains”

. . .

“underdeveloped speech uttered from the space between my organs”

. . .

“I sat down outside the laundromat and watched strangers walk by”

. . .

“steam rising out of the manhole covers”

. . .

“floating through fields of loose rock”

. . .

“what time is it?”

. . .

“everyone tall and looming”

. . .

ACT 65

"sun looming"
. . .
"Every movement my body makes is obscene"
. . .
"Beatboy perpetuates the woodland funeral march"
. . .
"shade flickering over edge of canopy"
. . .
"moon looming"
. . .
"there is no Wittgenstein who can appease me"
. . .
"slow drone of drum kit"
. . .
"Sun Ra arrives on my couch"
. . .
"light is conducte
. . .
"rockets are not laun

"with Wittg in har
. . .
"he asks m is what I h looking fo
. . .
"without a
. . .
"about betwee
. . .
"mention playing

"I attempt to reassemble."

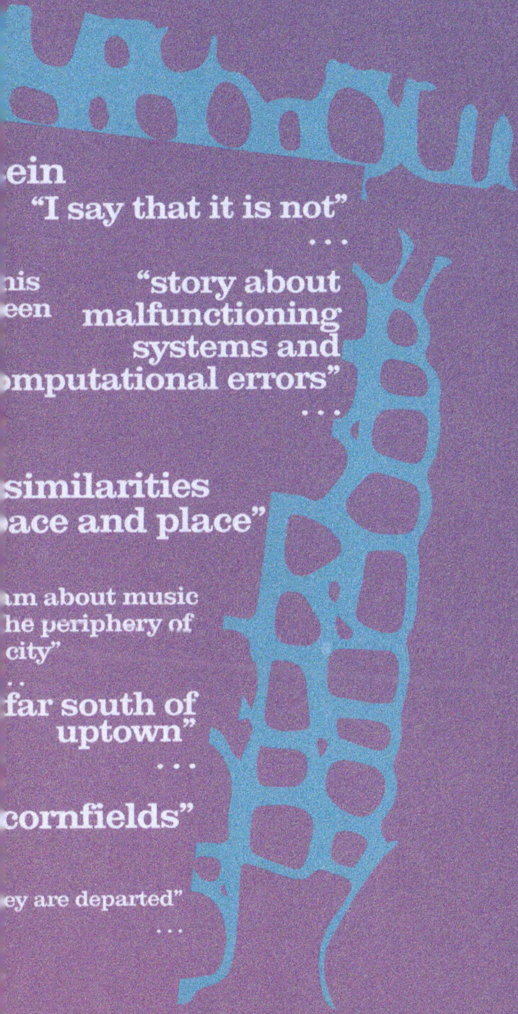

ein

"I say that it is not"

. . .

nis
een

"story about malfunctioning systems and
mputational errors"

. . .

similarities
ace and place"

m about music
he periphery of
city"

. .

far south of
uptown"

. . .

cornfields"

ey are departed"

. . .

"quietly zooming overhead"

"memories rising"

. . .

"they've been there"

"head swaying with melody"

. . .

"the horizon is obscured by flecks of black and white"

. . .

"your ass got to go"

. . .

"if they push that button"

. . .

. . .

"resurfacing I gasp for air"

. . .

"coming up out of the water"

. . .

"bathtub shattering into new fragments"

. . .

"not realizing where I have been"

. . .

"etc."

. . .

"nuclear war"

. . .

"dreams beginning their conception"

. . .

"he returns from space"

. . .

ACT 66

"Beatboy"
. . .

"he becomes unrecognizable"
. . .

"and undesirable"
. . .

"being and then nothingness."

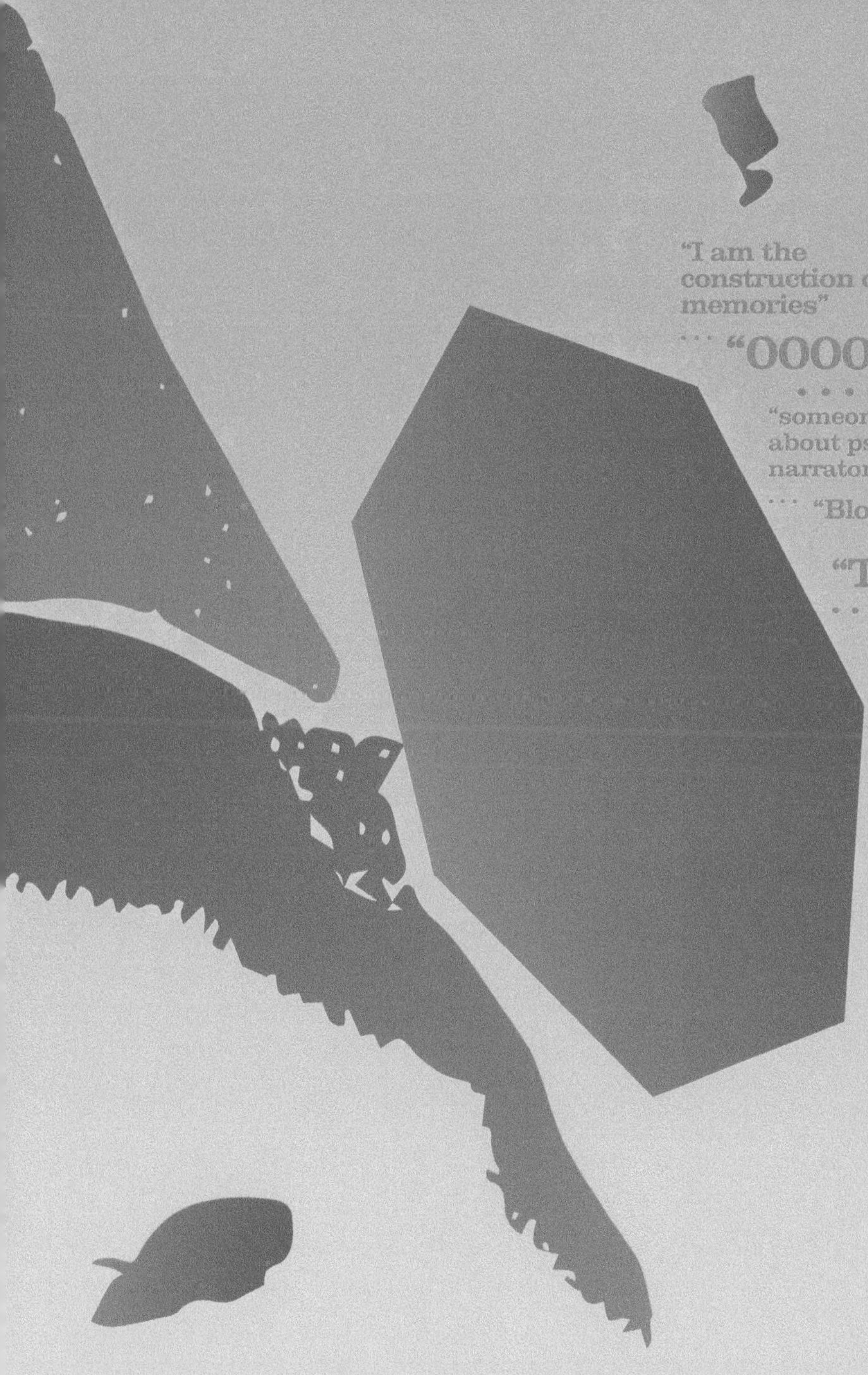

"I am the construction of my memories"

. . . "OOOOO"

• • •

"someone says something about psychogeography and the narrator-fool vomits"

. . . "Blondboy"

. . .

"Tommyboy"

• • •

"no more boys"

• • •

"no more dreams or deaths"

. . .

"the recreation of the past"

. . .

"abstractions are dragged into being"

. . .

• • •

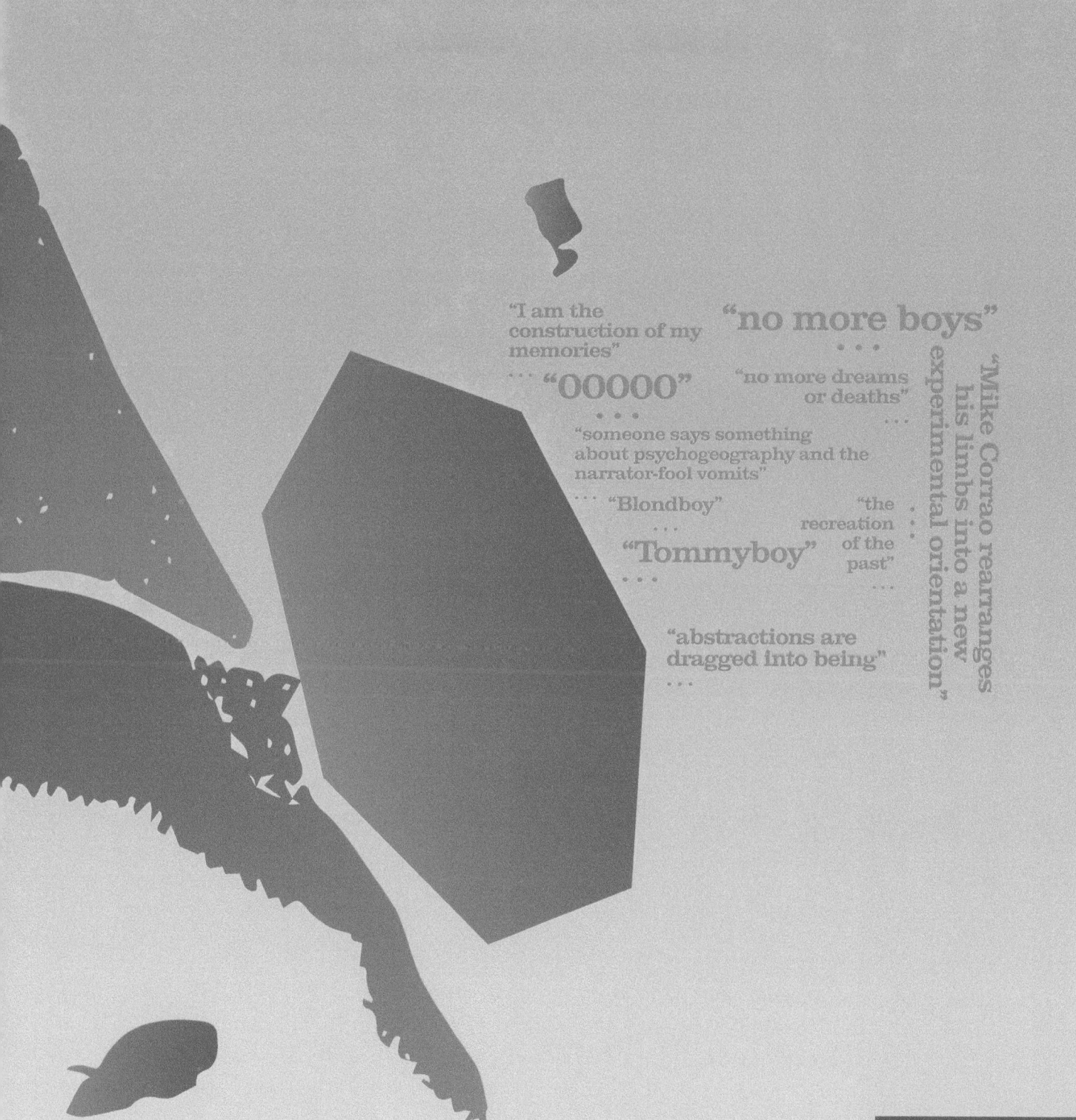

"Mike Corrao rearranges his limbs into a new experimental orientation"

ACT 67

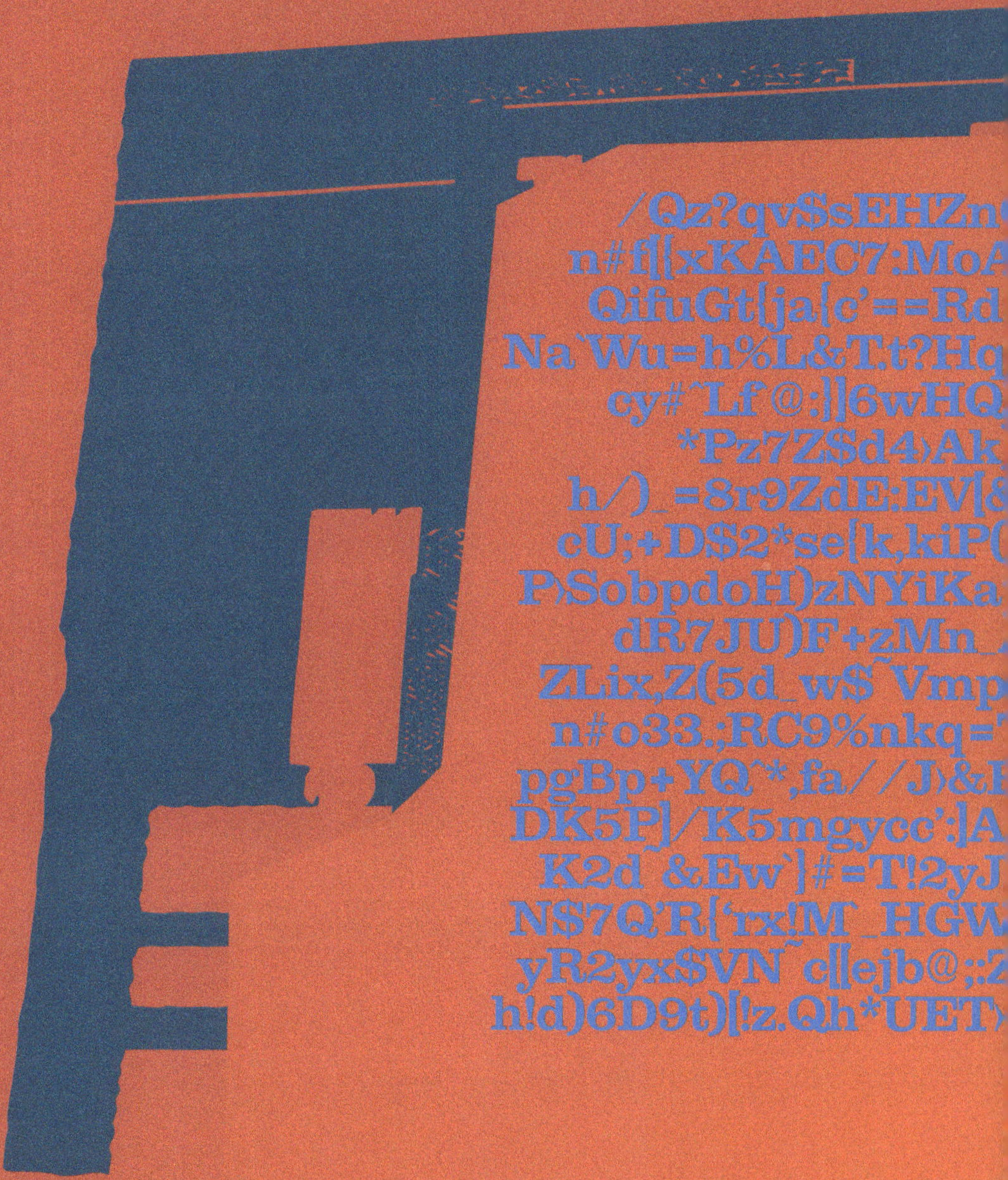
/Qz?qv$sEHZn
n#f[{xKAEC7:MoA
QifuGt{ja{c'==Rd
Na`Wu=h%L&T.t?Hq
cy#`Lf @;]]6wHQ
*Pz7Z$d4›Ak
h/)_=8r9ZdE:EV[8
cU;+D$2*se{k,kiP(
P›SobpdoH)zNYiKa
dR7JU)F+zMn_
ZLix,Z(5d_w$`Vmp
n#o33.;RC9%nkq=
pgBp+YQ^*,fa//J›&
DK5P]/K5mgycc':]A
K2d &Ew`}#=T!2yJ
N$7Q'R{'rx!M`_HGW
yR2yx$VN`c[[ejb@;;Z
h!d)6D9t)[!z.Qh*UET›

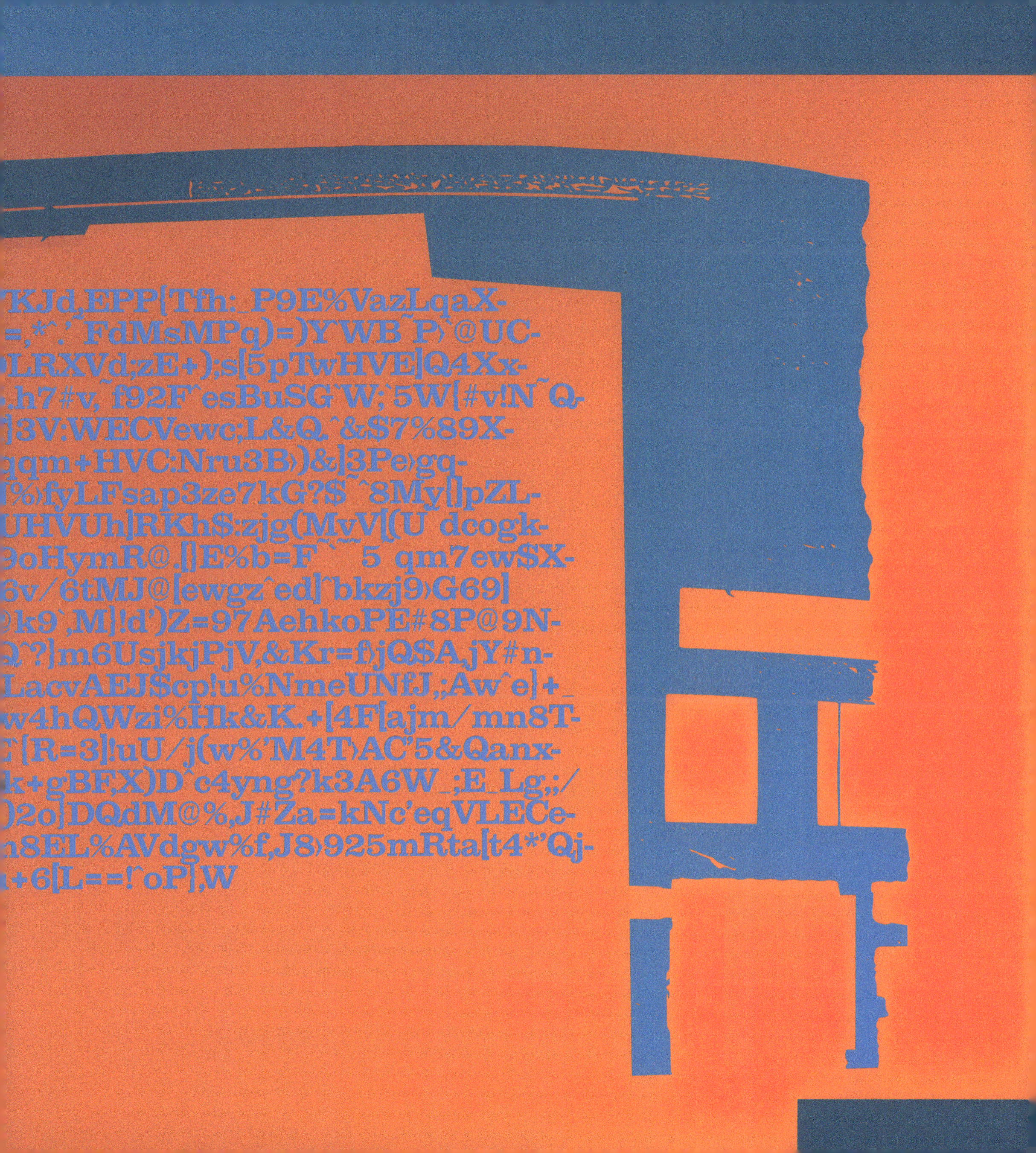
KJd,EPP{Tfh:_P9E%VazLqaX-
=,*^.' FdMsMPq)=)Y`WB~P›`@UC-
LRXVd;zE+);s[5pTwHVE]Q4Xx-
.h7#v, f92F^esBuSG`W;`5W{#v!N~Q-
}3V:WECVewc;L&Q.^&$7%89X-
qm+HVC:Nru3B›)&]3Pe›gq-
%›fyLFsap3ze7kG?$~^8My[]pZL-
UHVUh]RKh$:zjg(MvV[(U dcogk-
9oHymR@.[]E%b=F~`~ 5 qm7ew$X-
6v/6tMJ@[ewgz^ed]^bkzj9›G69]
k9`,M}!d')Z=97AehkoPE#8P@9N-
?}m6UsjkjPjV,&Kr=f›jQ$A,jY#n-
LacvAEJ$cp!u%NmeUNfJ,;Aw^e}+_
w4hQWzi%Hk&K.+[4F[ajm/mn8T-
{R=3]!uU/j(w%'M4T›AC'5&Qanx-
k+gBF,X)D^c4yng?k3A6W_;E_Lg,;/
)2o}DQdM@%,J#Za=kNc'eqVLECe-
n8EL%AVdgw%f,J8›925mRta[t4*'Qj-
+6[L==!^oP},W

ACT 68

~~"as an endless stream of voices rise"~~

...

"a new world is constructed from the static data"

...

"the delicate stacking of organs atop one another"

...

"which you have been accumulating"

...

"because you forgot to turn the sink off"

...

"residue derived from television monitors"

...

"the color isn't right"

...

"an obsolete artifact of a bygone era"

...

~~"our mouth is left ajar"~~

...

"the basement floods with water"

...

"each new voice from my mouth is recorded and stored"

...

"I am becoming ambient"

...

"drone not drones"

...

"I speak and then their echo replies"

...

"soft music of an incoherent voice"

...

"00000"

...

"sound of a car crash"

...

~~"through our throat and flood the room"~~

...

"Blondboy"

...

"Tommyboy"

...

"Beatboy"

...

"let's begin again"

. . .

"real people live in cities"

. . .

"in the laundry room"

. . .

"everywhere else is transitory"

. . .

"flecks of black and white"

. . .

"it is luminous and pink"

. . .

"you consult three exorcists"

. . .

"no one has the right answer"

. . .

"ooooo"

. . .

"radiation seeps into the wood and dissolves the dry wall"

. . .

"we consider moving out of uptown"

. . .

"it is not blue or clear or brown"

. . .

"or worse"

. . .

"it is permanent."

ACT 69

"Sun Ra lives on the other side of time"

. . .

"my existence becoming a multiplicity"

. . .

"when he visits my apartment"

. . .

"radiation carries across space"

. . .

"that he has learned to project himself as well"

. . .

"Adorno says that he is pleased with himself"

. . .

"the scene as it plays out at the polymer acropolis"

. . .

"time presents itself in duration"

. . .

"emanating from an obfuscated source"

. . .

"he says that he is not really here"

. . .

"an eventual and more comprehensive kind of decay"

. . .

(applause)

(laughter)

“that he has seen the forest”

• • • “this duration exhausts me”

. . .

“a row of teeth”

. . .

“a band of jazz musicians”

. . .

“when the ark is rebuilt”

. . .

“I am alone.”

ACT 70

ACT 71

"Blondboy"

. . .

"Tommyboy"

. . .

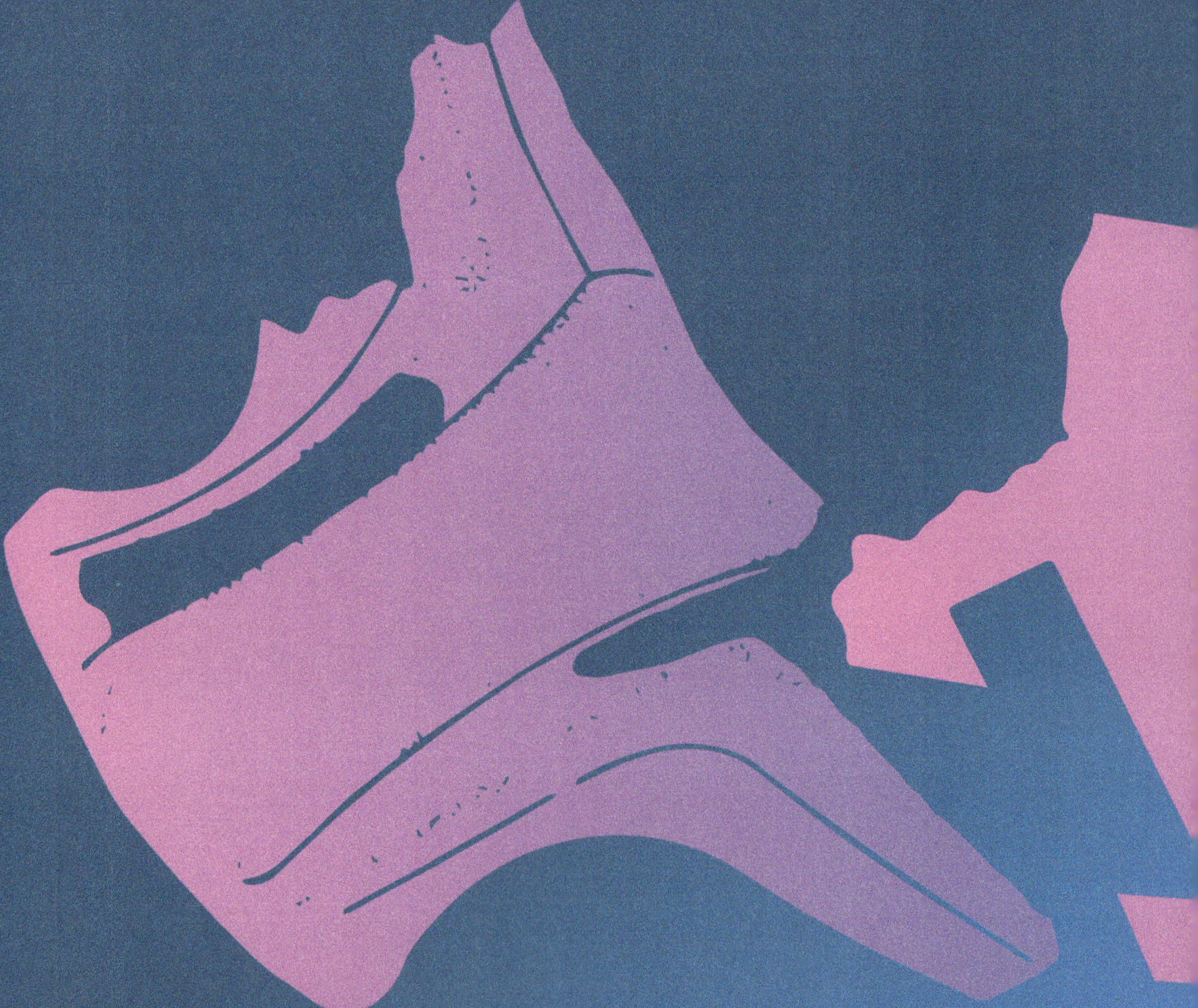

"Any memories?"

. . . "Blackblood flowing across porcelain"

. . .

"have you read the Wittgenstein?"

. . .

"how many strangers passed through the city?"

. . .

"a collage of bodies and architecture"

. . .

"with lair in the forest n of Antwerp"

. . .

"Beatboy"
. . .

"tome of the
minotaure"
. . .

"pleasurable
in its haptic
appeal"
. . .

"I do not
know
what to do
anymore."

"tell him that I
am sorry"
. . .

"Any dreams?"
. . .

lesh is poor
building
materials"
. . .

ACT 72

"You're gonna carry that weight."

ACKNOWLEDGEMENTS

Thank you Summer Freed, Olivia McCreary, Tyler Crumrine, Joe + Patty Corrao for your support and kindness.

Thank you John Trefry for your hardwork and incredible talent. This book could not exist without you.

26!

www.ingramcontent.com/pod-product-compliance
Lightning Source LLC
Chambersburg PA
CBHW042035100526
44587CB00030B/4430
9781732797178